GW00992264

Darkside Zodiac

in love

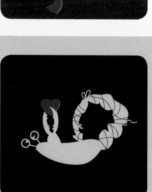

Darkside Zodiac
in love

Illustrated by
TONWEN JONES

Stella Hyde

**WEISER
BOOKS**

First published in 2007 by
Red Wheel/Weiser, LLC
With offices at:
500 Third Street, Suite 230
San Francisco, CA 94107
www.redwheelweiser.com

ISBN-10: 1-57863-415-6
ISBN-13: 978-1-57863-415-6

The dates for the zodiac signs in this book follow accepted standards, but people born at the
beginning or end of a sign should always check their birthchart; for technical, star-based reasons,
the start and end dates occasionally shift one day either way (and sometimes more), depending on the year.

Select passages from this book were previously published in *Darkside Zodiac*, Weiser Books, 2004.

This book was conceived, designed, and produced by iBall, an imprint of
IVY PRESS
The Old Candlemakers
West Street, Lewes
East Sussex, BN7 2NZ
United Kingdom

Creative Director *Peter Bridgewater*
Publisher *Jason Hook*
Editorial Director *Caroline Earle*
Senior Project Editor *Dominique Page*
Art Director *Sarah Howerd*
Designer and Illustrator *Tonwen Jones*

Cover photograph by Andrew Perris

Printed in Thailand

10 9 8 7 6 5 4 3 2 1

Contents

Introduction

There's no statistical backup for this, but it's a safe bet that most people check their horoscope to see if their soulmate is on the celestial horizon. Well, of course they're not—they can't fight their way past the crowds of conniving cheats, gold diggers, professional heartbreakers, and flaky meal-ticket junkies. Love makes fools of us all, and the USP of this book is that it shows you exactly how, from the first misguided glance to the last acrimonious injunction. Forewarned is forearmed.

There have been rumblings about other books in this series from people who don't seem to believe that the word "Darkside" in the title has any meaning. It does—you won't read anything flattering here, so if you want to frolic in eternal sunshine and you really believe that love is all you need, step away from this book.

How it works

Still with me? After a brief explanation of the Venus and Mars business, and some useful tips on the four signs with an unfair advantage in the game of love (Aries, Taurus, Libra, and Scorpio), we go straight into the signs. Each one follows the trajectory of a doomed love affair.

Starting with a lonely hearts ad that, for once, approximates to reality, we move on to discuss how your particular sign behaves: whether you favor the one-night stand, the two-year stretch, or the long haul; what your pickup lines are; and whether you are a stalker, a gold digger, or a tease.

Then we find out what dating you is like. Where do you score on the romance-o-meter? Where can the rest of us meet you, where would you take us, and what would we do? How are you about speed-dating? Are you better

off looking for romance cloaked in deep cyberspace? What sort of love token are you good for?

Things heat up as we approach the third date and find out what you are like between the sheets. Do you actually enjoy sex? What about your fantasies, your favorite moves, your most-used sex toy? How do you and Mars (the action planet, nudge, nudge) get along—if at all?

Next, to cool it down a little, we present you with Incompatibility Charts to show that nobody in the zodiac is a love match for you. Scales fall from your eyes, disillusionment sets in… So of course it all goes wrong, and we find out what kind of cheating dirtbag you really are, and whether you can even spell the word "commitment"; we put your conniving pre-nup under the microscope, and listen to your ridiculous excuses. There are tips on how the rest of us can get back at you, but they'll hardly dent your love-rat armor.

Finally—because there has to be some possibility of things getting better, even on the Darkside—we show how you and Venus get it together, and offer a couple of hot, inspirational signmates, to help you forget what a pig's breakfast you made of it last time and convince yourself that of course you could be a contender again; it's called the triumph of hope over experience.

Instant blind-date identifier

At the end of the book, as a special service to readers, you'll find the *Darkside Zodiac* Instant Blind-Date Identifier. Take this handy guide with you and consult it under the table; it will help you discover your BD's sign without having to ask for their birthday, so that you can decide whether to escape via the restroom window a.s.a.p. or hang around until they have paid the check.

Venus and Mars

You may think you know that men are from Mars, and women are from Venus. Do not be upset if I tell you this is not true—just the result of marketing's infatuation with alliteration. All of us, of all genders, have a stake in both planets: Venus is the girlie planet of lurve (although any innocent who believes she is all about soft fluffiness and doe-eyed adoration is in for a shock) and Mars is planet thrust. Venus brings desire and harmony, Mars brings energy and drive. They are the zodiac's twin love/lust drive. So you see, where these two menaces are in your birthchart has consequences, especially for the Darkside.

You may think your sun sign makes you an irresistible tease, but Venus in a chilly sign will cut you off at the knees; you may think you are a babe magnet, but Mars in a timid sign leaves you standing awkward and tongue-tied at the wrong end of the bar. Get hold of a birthchart before you make any more mistakes. If you go to www.alabe.com armed only with your birth date and, if possible, time and place of birth, you can get a free computer-generated chart showing exactly what Venus and Mars were getting up to when you were born.

Venus and you

Venus is far too luxury-loving to move too far away from the Sun (Big Daddy), and its orbital rate is in bed with Earth's, so Earth and Venus are spinning around the Sun in a kind of celestial embrace (or, on the Darkside, the deathgrip that goes with an acrimonious divorce). This means that, for complicated astrophysical reasons we don't need to understand, it only ever appears in your sun sign, or

two signs on either side of it. So if you are a tough-minded Capricorn, there is no way your Venus can make up for it by showing up in caring Cancer. (Geminis need careful watching here, in case they claim a Venus in a solid sign nowhere near them, but now that you know, you can nip this kind of thing in the bud.)

Each sign contains a section on Venus and how she affects it. We tell you how Venus relates to your sign, and where else she could possibly be flirting/cheating/sulking in your chart, and what this might mean. It's not always pretty.

Mars and you

More usually found fomenting unrest and invading sovereign nations for their own good, Mars on the battlefield of love is the one that enables you to overcome shyness, sense, decorum, suitability, etc. and go for someone way out of your league. It's also the one that, in the wrong place, gets you a rapsheet. A small note about Mars appears in the "Sex with…" section for each sign, explaining how Mars affects your sign. Because Mars can leap out of ambush anywhere, this is where it pays to get a birthchart. If you discover where your Mars is, and it's different from your sun sign, consult that sign in this book. For example, if you are a Leo and your Mars is in Aquarius, consult the Aquarius section to find out why you don't seem to care as much as you should when your advances are ignored.

Venus the planet

Venus is the second rock from the Sun, our nearest neighbor, and the planet most like Earth. It orbits just that little bit faster than we do, and on the inside lane. Astros often call it our sister planet and drone on about how harmonious and lovely it is gliding alongside us, looking pale and luminous. Obviously these are astros without sisters of their own. Venus will not be rushed out of bed. It has the slowest rotation rate in the solar system, taking 243 Earth days to make one languorous twirl on its own axis. That is longer than it takes for it to go around the Sun (225 days), so you can see you are dealing with class-A langour here. And it spins clockwise, unlike any other planet, just because it can. Somehow it is no surprise that it is the brightest natural object in the night sky (apart from the Moon) and insists on being uptitled as both the Morning Star and Evening Star.

Mars the planet

Mars is the fourth rock from the Sun. It's the glowering red psychopath that orbits on our outside lane (so with Venus on the inside, Earth is always and everywhere caught between Love and War; neat, huh?). Mars is only half our size, but that doesn't really help. It stalks our orbit at half speed, taking about two and a half years to get around, so it can spend a couple of months of quality menacing time in each sign, and we can always see it just out of the corner of our eye. It has two lumpy henchmoons called Phobos (Mr. Fear) and Deimos (Mr. Loathing).

Venus the goddess

Venus is the only important celestial object named for a goddess (apart from some negligible minor moons and asteroids). This is the Roman goddess of love and harmony, the lite version of Greek Aphrodite, the flint-hearted tease who went through lovers (gods and human) like a stiletto through chocolate mousse; renowned for going after the many objects of her desire with a singularity of passion and purpose that is admired and emulated by land-grabbing evil emperors, asset strippers, and eight-year-old girls everywhere. She was the daughter of Zeus, and not to be messed with, so don't start now.

Mars the god

Mars is named for the Roman god of war. Adored and worshipped by the Roman army, he was a remix of an ancient agricultural god and Ares, the Greek god of war (well, fighting)—a loud-mouthed, violent braggart who was easily outclassed on Olympus by his sister Athena (goddess of war with wisdom).

Taking Advantage

All is not fair in love (or war). If you think of Venus and Mars as the prom queen and top jock of the zodiac, then four particular signs—Aries, Taurus, Libra, and Scorpio—are like their best friends or posse, because Venus rules Taurus and Libra, and Mars

Aries

Advantage: a natural-born red-hot lover, or think they are, which is much the same thing.

This is a masculine cardinal Fire sign, than which you cannot get much more Yang. It is also ruled by Mars, in his conquering-hero, blood-spattered gladiator role. This means that Aries subjects approach the whole love/lust thing with the boundless confidence of a self-accredited alpha male—even when they aren't. Amazingly, they get away with it for most of the time, regardless of looks, talent, credit rating, personality, or dress sense. Failure is never an option; when spurned, Aries subjects simply focus on an easier target, and are never found repining, regretting, or apologizing.

Taurus

Advantage: always get their man or woman, along with their own way—and anything else they want.

This is a feminine fixed Earth sign, ruled by Venus in her material-girl avatar. Taurus subjects know exactly what they want, and very little will stop them getting it; they never have doubts and they don't mind waiting. So when they fall for someone and go after them, they've got the goddess of grab-and-hold on their side. And because they know that when money flies out of the window, love goes with it, they will not put up with an insubstantial love token. You will not find them starving for love, or sighing about the one that got away, because no one whom Taurus really wants can ever get away.

rules Aries and still has influence over Scorpio. So if you are Aries, Taurus, Libra, or Scorpio, you have a bit of an edge when it comes to love and lust; it looks like an unfair advantage to the rest of us. It is. Here's how.

Libra

Advantage: know instinctively how to make love for fun and profit without giving their heart away.

This is a masculine cardinal Air sign and is ruled by Venus in her whimsical, manipulative mode (the mood that saw her starting the Trojan War in a fit of pique). This explains the irresistible gigolo aspect of Libra (regardless of actual gender) and why Librans can charm anyone into bed (or, even better, Bloomies) and have their delicious way with them, then change their mind, abandon them when something better comes along, and yet somehow avoid any acid reflux. You will not find Librans crying over spilt lovers, because that would make them blotchy, which would be unfair on the next client.

Scorpio

Advantage: totally justified Brightside and Darkside rep as the sexiest sign in the zodiac.

This is a feminine fixed Water sign once ruled by Mars (Scorpio is like the quiet, cool one in any group, who runs off to the big city to make his fortune—in this case with Pluto). However, early influences don't fade, and Scorpio subjects can thank Mars for their diploma in the art of war between the sexes, and for all the hot lust that seethes below the ice-cool exterior; that plus the fact that Scorpio is the sign that rules the genitals. Scorpios never give up control, so you will never find them martyring themselves in a failing relationship—unless, of course, they have chosen to.

The Signs

Aries

March 21–April 19

Tired of boring old consensual relationships?
Looking for someone to sweep you off your feet
(literally), take over your life for as long as it suits
me, cut you off from friends and family with my
relentless psychotic jealous rages, then dump you,
for no apparent reason—and probably in the ER?
Extremely assertive, unjustifiably superconfident,
self-certified action hero(ine) available anytime,
anywhere, WLTM anyone with a pulse. Present
circumstances irrelevant, as I won't listen to a word
you say, but don't call me if you like quiet evenings
in with chamomile tea and Joanna Newsom.

One-night stand

The Aries love-maneuver of choice; it's a big old world out there, and a hell of a lot of people to get through and share the wonder that is you. Partners should be grateful: one night is a very long time on the Aries clock, and could count as total commitment, looked at from some angles.

Two-year stretch

This will only work if Aries is in uniform (very likely) and on a long tour of duty somewhere far away, or on the road in their big red truck. It will look like two years on paper, but you only have to spend 24 hours actually together in the same room, or even the same state.

Long-haul

Mission Impossible. No Aries can stay on that long. If trapped, you could take the Aries way out (rage-induced coronary, blowing self up on barbecue, etc.) and, because you never do paperwork, there's no insurance payola for the partner who dared to trap you, ha-ha.

Aries in Love

hot pursuit

No one could miss an Aries in love. It's like being in a cheesy musical where the juve lead grabs innocent bystanders by the throat and bellows his most delicate, inexpressibly intimate feelings into their faces, before leading an energetic bump-and-grind chorus to ram the point home. You bring all the focus and determination of a tomcat to your relationship—and about as much commitment. All your energy goes into the pursuit, and the thrill of beating off the competition (this is often mistaken for jealousy). When you have won, you are insanely possessive, but it doesn't last because, although you fall in love hard and often, you fall out of love just as frequently, a few hours later.

Stalker?

Technically, for the few days that love burns, but victims shouldn't bother with a restraining order because you will be off after fresh meat before it can get served.

Tease?

Regardless of gender, you're strictly caveman. It would be a subtlety too far to promise what you don't plan to deliver.

Gold digger?

You're an equal-ops lover; anyway, your energy levels would kill any ancient zillionaire before the pre-nup was signed.

Ram pickup lines

Forget wit or innovation, or even a line vaguely tailored to the love object's personality. You're still stuck on:
- ♥ How d'you like your eggs in the morning?
- ♥ Me Tarzan
- ♥ Hoo-rah!

Dating Aries
the thrill of the chase

Dating is just social hunting, right?—without the kill shot—and there's nothing you like better. Not getting a date is not an Aries option. You are persistent, insensitive, and have no problem with lowering your standards, so in the end most people give in just to shut you up, because once you've downed the prey, the game is half over. What you really like is going after a juicy target in competition with your best buddy; stealing the prize from under their noses is what really turns you on, and you give yourself extra points if the prize is someone your best buddy really, really likes.

The trouble is, with your kill rate, you can seriously deplete dating stock, so you're eternally grateful to Rabbi Yaacov Deyo, the inventor of speed-dating, a time-saving system that combines quantity and turnover in a way you can only describe as awesome.

You'll hunt anywhere, but Aries junkies know you can usually be found where there is fire, metal, guns, cars, sweat, or danger, or hanging out with the guys at your local waterhole, talking about past glories.

During the dating period you are oppressively ardent, bombarding the target with giant bouquets and beaming hourly shots of yourself looking soulful to their cellphones. If you're not already a bike messenger, you'll dress up as one and deliver giant cuddly toys just as they are closing that career-clinching deal.

You take your date where you want to go: the steakhouse where all your buddies hang, a demo derby perhaps, or a Metallica gig. You pay the first time, usually in cash, because your plastic has been called in/singed/lost. It won't occur to you to call again after the third date. What would be the point?

Aries love token

You have a totally unjustified rep for boundless generosity, because any love token you give in the heat of the chase will be something you really, really want yourself. That way, when you and your lover break up, and they throw it back at you in disgust, you still win; so that'll be a Ferrari Testarossa then, or at least a Rolex Oyster.

Romance Levels

- incandescent
- burning
- hot
- warm
- cool
- cold
- sub-zero

Aries online

Although a bit heavy-hooved on the hardware (how many keyboards do you go through in a week?), you love cyberdating, because it matches with your carpet-bomb approach: cover all bases, you are bound to hit something. So you've signed up to all the online dating sites, regardless of orientation, and have just discovered MySpace—what an Arien concept, a space all about me! You spoil it a bit by telling the truth in your résumé, because you don't really understand about spin and marketing.

21

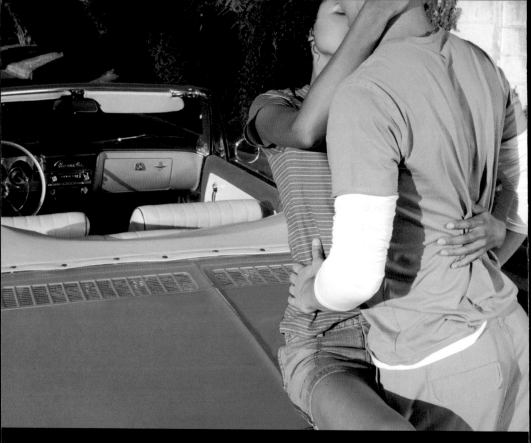

What gets Aries hot

Because you are good to go anytime, anywhere, with whoever's standing next in line, partners don't have to do much more than breathe. However, lovers who turn up in uniform (even if it's just the pizza boy's) and a Hummer® will definitely have your attention. Role-play is a bit complex; you get much more trigger happy doing it for real, snatching wordless moments under the dark moon during downtime on night maneuvers with your National Guard Platoon.

Between the sheets

On top. Are there other ways? It's direct, simple, and easy to get off when you're done and it's time to move on. Plus you can easily keep an eye on the stopwatch hanging on the bedpost that you use for your personal time trials. Even if the earth remains stationary, you are guaranteed a free workout that will really boost your upper arm strength. Any flat surface will do (rug burn comes with the territory), bedroom or barnyard, it's all the same to you.

Sɛχ ꭐitꜰ Arıεş

hard and fast

The rest of us may think of sex as the sublime union of soul and spirit expressed through physical ecstasy, but you think of it as an extreme sport, as it involves exercise, stamina, competition, and a prize. Lust does not slow you down or quench your competitive spirit—you're strictly a notches-on-the-bedpost kinda guy (or girl). You have to do it harder, faster, and quicker than everyone else, and of course you always have to come first. You'll try to get to home plate on date—that's the name of the game, isn't it?—but if you don't, it's respect to your opponent for great defensive play, 24 hours to regroup, then you try again, and harder. You don't do regrets (you don't have that much of a long-term memory) and, because you are in constant training, you're always up for it (none of this headache business) and enjoy frequent-flier status at the STD clinic.

Aries and Mars

As you know (*see page 9*), Mars is the patron planet of thrust, so where Mars is strutting in your birthchart will determine whether your sex drive is automatic, stick shift, or turbo. Aries is ruled by Mars, so if your Mars is in Aries as well as your Sun, you are a double-barreled sex machine with extra libido tanks; if not already locked up as a sex pest, you soon will be.

Aries sex toys

What for? All that stuff with handcuffs and honey just slows you down. And your Rampant Rabbit hasn't worked since you used it to jump-start the Ducati. A replica AK-47 for hostage games could be fun.

Incompatibility Charts

aries vs. the rest

Brightsiders say that Aries (masculine, Fire, cardinal, psychopath) gets along best with other Fire signs who'll understand (Leo and Sagittarius), and worst with Libra, Cancer, and Capricorn (the other cardinal signs who also want to rule the roost). However, this is the Darkside, where everybody is incompatible with everyone else. Here's how.

Aries and Aries Hot, violent, and shortlived; when you run out of ammo, you both move on to new killing fields with no hard feelings, but it takes the rest of the zodiac years to clear up the rubble.

Aries and Taurus Remember what you learned about irresistible forces and immovable objects, and what happens when they meet? Something has to give—probably the fabric of the universe.

Aries and Gemini This relationship is the model for the Beauty and the Beast fairytale. Guess who is what! You know you'll end up dead or as the Dancing Bear in their circus, but you can't resist.

Aries and Cancer Another cardinal sign, passive to your aggressive. It all goes wrong when they crash your gang meet to bring you lunch and show you the drape samples they've chosen.

Aries and Leo A fellow Fire sign, but fixed, so impatient, energetic, stubborn, yet focused; they will fight you for the Pants of Power and you may not win, because they are smarter than you.

Aries and Virgo Filling in a risk-assessment form before every date, and being nagged to shreds whenever you forget an insignificant detail like their birthday, soon cools this one down.

24

Aries and Libra You are Stanley Kowalski, they are Stella DuBois. They make you feel so sweaty you forget they are: a) your opposite sign, and b) another cardinal sign—and after your wallet.

Aries and Scorpio You'll do anything they say, which is why you were found with the blood-covered knife in your hand and the body of their ex at your feet, and are now in a correctional facility.

Aries and Sagittarius The last Fire sign, a headstrong, risk-addicted soulmate; great while it lasts, until you both go over a cliff or down in a blaze of bullets from the sheriff's posse.

Aries and Capricorn The last cardinal sign of the zodiac, so a threat. Fortunately, they want nothing to do with you because they're afraid their insurance premiums will go up.

Aries and Aquarius A primitive, unreconstructed specimen like you will intrigue them for several days, but when they work out that you only have the one trick, they throw you back in the pond.

Aries and Pisces They cling on to you, because you are all action and they are all wet; your well-honed survival instinct lets you shake them off before they cut your hair and sap your strength.

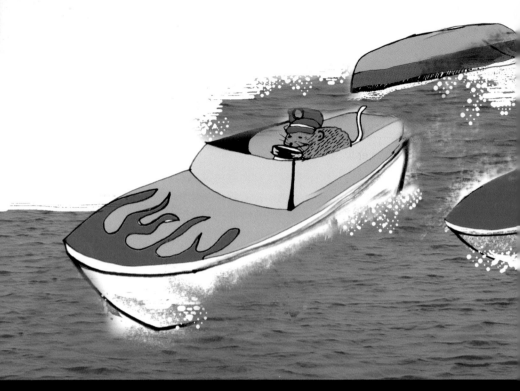

Love rat?

The worst kind: übercompetitive and insensitive at the same time. It's the winning, and the beating off rivals, and bucking overwhelming odds (they are Amish, you are a Texas Ranger; they are claustrophobic, you are a caver, etc.) that float your boat. Once you've won the prize, it isn't what you want anymore, so you trash the relationship (so that rivals can't use it) and get away as fast as you can, without a backward glance at the wreckage you leave behind.

GETTING BACK AT ARIES

Note to rest of zodiac: do not waste your time on deliciously byzantine revenge plots to make Aries feel the pain. Dump sugar in their SUV gas tank if it makes you feel better, but Aries will just rant and blame everyone but you, because they will have completely wiped you from their mind.

Your Cheatin' Heart
serial killer

Look, you are a serial lover with a fast turnover (often hourly), not a devious cheat. You do so do commitment, but in very small and intense packets that can only be measured in nanosecs—sort of quantum commitment. Relationships never last long enough to get to the "we need to talk" stage, which is good as you have no idea what this means— what would you say?—and you've never really wanted to hear anything from the beloved completely comatose is good in your book). When you dump, you give exact and complete reasons, so they understand where they went wrong and how to up their game next time. It's the kind of tip you would appreciate, if you weren't already the best you could be. If your lover cheats on you, you follow them home with a baseball bat or a samurai sword to avenge your honor.

Aries excuses

Never apologize, never explain; no excuse, baby, no surrender. So you're late, smell strangely musky, and are covered in hickeys and nail marks; so what? You never say, "It's not you, it's me," because it isn't. And you never say, "I just need more space"; you just leave.

Aries pre-nup

There probably won't be an actual pre-nup because you will inevitably lose the paperwork, but this is what you expect partners to do: agree with every word you say, never criticize anything you do, leave all major life decisions to you, let you do exactly what you want when you want, but not expect you to do anything they want, and not to get boring and difficult when you leave them.

Venus and Aries

i'm a lover and a fighter

Don't think that just because you are Aries you can stay in the bar with the boys and avoid the girly planet. According to Greek myth, Venus has Mars wrapped around her manicured pinkie, and Mars is your ruler. This means you are regularly led astray by lust, but it's never your fault—you are putty in Venus's mitt. Astrological logistics (*see pages 8–9*) mean that your Venus will be in Aries, Aquarius, Pisces, Taurus, or Gemini.

Hot Aries Role Models

Giacomo Casanova, April 2, 1725
Alpha-class poster boy for serial lovers. Ensured consistently high hit rate by moving around a lot; final score: 122.

Bette Davis, April 5, 1908
Combative Hollywood player with a forceful personality that served her better than conventional beauty; got through four marriages and three divorces.

Venus in Aries

Venus in Aries, when you are already Aries, is a recipe for GSR on the sheets, multiple stalking convictions, and maybe a stretch for abduction. You always get your man (or woman), often at gunpoint, and you're a tough love fanatic: handcuffs, whips, pain, etc.—and that's just when you're on your own. You always hurt the one you love, on principle.

Venus in Aquarius

Fewer arrests with this placing, because Aquarius is way cooler, and gives you a few minutes' longer attention span. You know better than to charge at the love target with all flags waving; you have cunning plans involving decoys and playing dead.

Venus in Pisces

Venus is the manipulation queen, and the manipulation mother lode runs through Pisces; so you come on classic tough, but vulnerable, faking a war wound or a dueling scar (so romantic) or three, to incite pity and admiration in your target. You know there's nothing more alluring than a wounded hero— even though you aren't one.

Venus in Taurus

Venus rules Taurus, so although tough, you want your prey live and pretty, not dead on a slab like Romeo. So your ammo of choice is trank darts, so that your target wakes up unharmed in your very cozy prisoner-of-love nest.

Venus in Gemini

Venus in Gemini means an even itchier trigger finger. So it's heavy-duty extreme flirting, usually while bear hunting, base jumping, gun running, or liberating small countries, and generally with the whole platoon. You know you are irresistible in distressed combats.

Taurus

April 20–May 20

Looking for real security? Long, long evenings in by the fire, with just the two of us comparing pension plans and checking bank statements? Are you handsome, solvent, and allergic to change? Stubborn upholder of traditional values, with own comfort zone and a penchant for sticky mud, WLTM that special someone who prefers standing still to moving and who appreciates a predictable, set-in-stone routine, will be an asset in my portfolio of love, and wants to be really looked after. Every breath you take, I promise to be watching you. Don't call if you don't like chocolate or don't appreciate the occasional murderous rage.

One-night stand

Only very young bulls have the flexibility for this, because it requires spontaneity and speedy reflexes. The concept of doing anything just once does not compute (no return on initial investment), and you get distressed when you go back the next night and the love object is not there.

Two-year stretch

This is just a little bit fast and furious for your liking. Two years is a mere blip in the scheme of things, barely enough time to get your lover used to your intractable little ways; it would be wasteful and flighty to end it all just as you had both settled into a really satisfactory routine.

Long-haul

This is exactly the kind of thing you like. Hauling heavy loads around in circles? Plowing the same furrow year on year? Lead you to it! Everything—including your partner—tied down securely, roses around your door, picket fence around your land, and death the only way out.

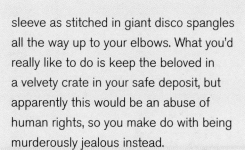

Taurus in Love
having and holding

Love is just another name for territorial expansion, laying claim to more stuff, so you fall in love regularly, and carry on being in love unless diverted by something substantial, like a meteor strike in your home state. We all know when you are in love because you are appallingly smug and self-satisfied about it, stand far too close to the love object breathing heavily, do a lot of pawing, and wear your heart not so much on your sleeve as stitched in giant disco spangles all the way up to your elbows. What you'd really like to do is keep the beloved in a velvety crate in your safe deposit, but apparently this would be an abuse of human rights, so you make do with being murderously jealous instead.

Stalker?
Five-star. Surveillance the CIA would kill for, and a homing device built into the birthday Bulgari; it's not stalking—it's protecting your investment.

Tease?
If only. You always do exactly what you say you will do. Who wants surprises?

Gold digger?
Not really; you just like to be sure that they've got enough stuff of their own not to be lusting after your stuff.

Bull pickup lines

You are still using the pickup lines you had as a bullock:
- ♥ What's your favorite candy?
- ♥ Want to see my pension plan?
- ♥ How you doin'?

Dating Taurus

let's eat

You will always get a date, partly because most of you are quite cute—in a solid, thick-necked way—but mostly because you are relentlessly persistent. When you meet someone you like, you think of them as you do the rest of your stuff (you love stuff). Nothing stands in the way of you and your stuff, so you just keep charging at the gate until it gives way, or stand and bellow until you get what you want. It usually works.

You often suffer from dry patches because you hate leaving your comfort zone (where you have already dated everybody) to try out the hot new singles bar at the other end of town, but speed-dating sometimes gets you through the night. Ignore the word "speed," and concentrate on the methodology. Two minutes' fascinating conversation is about as much as you can manage in one night, and you have no problem repeating the same thing 30 times in succession to 30 different hopefuls. What's even better is that they're all in one place, so you don't have to move around too much—and there are nibbles.

If the rest of the zodiac want to bag a Taurus, all they have to do is go to the mall or, for something a little more upmarket, hang around the truffle counter at Dean & DeLuca's.

Datees don't get much say in the choice of venue or entertainment. On the first date you go to your favorite diner. You don't need to pay—it goes on your tab. On the second date you go to your favorite diner (things can get very tense if you are both Taurean). On the third date you go to your favorite diner and then back to your slightly overheated apartment with a doggy bag. Will you call again? Hell, yes, every day, at the same time until they get their number delisted.

Romance Levels

- incandescent
- burning
- hot
- warm
- cool
- cold
- sub-zero

Taurus love token

Traditional is best, so it's flowers and candy, even though your date has hay fever and is diabetic. Wealthy bulls have a discreet arrangement with Tiffany's or Bloomie's, which hold a stock of tasteful, yet identical bracelets/cufflinks to be sent out as thank-you gifts whenever Taurus gets lucky.

Taurus online

Although not one of nature's early adopters, you like online dating because you can browse through the merchandise from the comfort of your own recliner with a gallon of Ben & Jerry's Chocolate Chip Cookie Dough in one hand and a magnum of Margaux in the other. It's like leafing through a Williams-Sonoma catalog. You like Natural Selection best because it has traditional values: the men pay, and have to be loaded; the women go free, and have to be beautiful; so everyone knows exactly where they stand.

What gets Taurus hot

Apart from being a bit lookist, you're easily pleased. Fantasies are not you; you like something you can get hold of and chew. You'll roll over for anyone swathed in leather and cashmere who brings their own neroli massage oil and whispers dirty money in your ears (ring-fenced offshore trust funds ... high-end leveraged buyout ... currency arbitrage). And anyone who turns up with a luxury picnic hamper (even if you are not planning to go out) is onto a very sure thing.

Between the sheets

Missionary, what else? It's tried, tested, and traditional, and keeps your hands free so that you can reach out for candy whenever you want. It also means you are lying down and can move as slowly as you like. Lovers who try to inject a little novelty or spontaneity into proceedings come up against your implacable resistance to change and end up using the Kama Sutra as a coaster to prevent the bucket of chocolate body paint making marks on your pristine parquet.

Sex with Taurus

slow and steady

Allegedly, you are sensuous, languorous, and lollingly delicious between the sheets, and are much sought-after for your awesome stamina and legendary slow hoof. You are appreciated (for a short time) by people who have been, say, bungee-humping with Sagittarius, but you can have too much of a good thing. The trouble is that once you have learned how to make the earth move (in your case, by standing still and moving up and down on the spot for a couple of hours), you just keep getting into the same old groove. It gives a whole new meaning to the word "rutting." You find that partners often fall asleep after the regulation 10 minutes (maybe those were groans of boredom, not whimpers of desire), but this doesn't bother you because it means you don't have to talk afterward and can get on with your post-coital donut and latte in peace.

Taurus and Mars

As you have discovered (*see page 9*), Mars is the planet of thrust, and wherever it stands in your birthchart will determine whether your sex drive is meatloaf, hamburger, or fillet steak. Mars is in detriment in Taurus, which means that its power is kind of diminished, or at least not on full-beam. If your Mars is in Taurus, as well as your Sun, this can only be good, because who would want to be jumped by 400 pounds of lust-crazed pot roast?

Taurus sex toys

So chocolate body paint is a cliché ... but you like clichés, and you like chocolate body paint—with a large brush so you can express your artistic temperament and get more in your mouth.

Incompatibility Charts

taurus vs. the rest

Brightsiders say that Taurus (feminine, Earth, fixed, oral-fixated) gets along best with other Earth signs who'll understand (Virgo and Capricorn), and worst with Leo, Scorpio, and Aquarius (the other fixed signs who see obstinacy as a virtue). However, this is the Darkside, where everybody is incompatible with everyone else. Here's how.

Taurus and Aries They can't resist testing whether that red-rag-and-bull stuff really works, because it's such fun watching you explode into one of your murderous rages. Who needs it?

Taurus and Taurus You might plod along side by side in cozy bovine indifference for years until you disagree about who owns the chocolate fountain, then it all goes Kramer vs. Kramer.

Taurus and Gemini Death in the afternoon. Bedazzling in their suit of lights, they'll twinkle about and make mincemeat of you, and you'll be lucky to come out of it with your ears still on.

Taurus and Cancer You think they're being quiet and contented, but they're heaping up grudges about slights you can't begin to remember, then they run away sideways so you can't follow.

Taurus and Leo Another fixed sign, determined to hog center stage and wear the crown; however, they will kindly let you be the impresario so that you can bankroll their glorious enterprise.

Taurus and Virgo Another Earth sign, but mutable, so constantly fidgeting (you prefer standing still) and, even worse, replacing your routine with theirs, and making you eat in Other Restaurants.

Taurus and Libra Although you two share a planetary ruler (Venus), it does not bring harmony and cooing, but fights to the death over who used up the last of your Coco de Mer body lotion.

Taurus and Scorpio Your opposite, and another fixed sign, so just as implacably jealous and possessive; the pair most likely to be found locked in a death grip in a pool of cake crumbs.

Taurus and Sagittarius All that loud noise and sudden movement makes you extremely tetchy, so it's just as well they have come and gone before you get into one of your homicidal rages.

Taurus and Capricorn They may be an Earth sign, and it's fun talking dirty about high-interest savings accounts, but they sneer at your gold bath accessories and have no grasp on luxury shopping.

Taurus and Aquarius The last fixed sign. Doomed, because you are stubborn, but they are stubborn and contrary; you say tomato, they say tomahto, you say potato, they say starchy edible tuber.

Taurus and Pisces Every night they spin you a different entertaining tale to explain why they are late; one morning you are going to wake up from your torpor and have them beheaded.

Love rat?

Love ratting is not your sport. When you've got something or somebody, you hang on to it or them. If you are caught with your pants down, it will be because shiny-tongued Gemini has fogged your brain with chocolate and red wine, and made a move on you and your assets. You only understand what's going on when your irate lover shows you the snapshots on Gawker and it's all too late.

GETTING BACK AT TAURUS

Note to other signs: don't bother with witty comebacks or smart pranks—anything that subtle will fly straight over the horns. If you really want to rile a Taurus (they are a sitting target, after all), get them banned from their favorite restaurant by posting a libelous review in their name on salon.com.

Your Cheatin' Heart

why bother?

Since you need to make a very large turning circle before you can set off in another direction, and you hate change, you're not famous for cheating or dumping. In fact, you are a bit dense when it comes to being dumped (why would anyone want to dump you, just when you'd got them used to your routine and were so comfortable that you no longer even had to talk?). You think "I need more space" means let's buy a bigger field. You don't like dumping (it ruins your routine), but if your financial advisor says you need to dump, you do it by standing still and pawing the ground in an annoying manner until your partner leaves. To stop your partner cheating on you, you weigh them down with golden handcuffs. Many of you never reach this stage because you suffer from a chronic disinclination to commit (*Clooneyitis irritans*).

Taurus excuses

You don't have the imagination to make excuses; you are so rarely where you shouldn't be. In the unlikely event of an extracurricular activity, your partner already knows about it (it's in your diary) and is probably grateful to have someone else along to share the load.

Taurus pre-nup

You never leave the field without a pre-nup, even if it's only the second date. Not only does the Taurus pre-nup ironclad your stuff, but it also lays out exactly what, how, and when you and the loved one will do, say, and eat for the duration of the relationship: where you will live, when you will have sex, when you will have children, and, probably, when you will die. Only then can you relax.

Venus and Taurus
mighty aphrodite

Venus rules Taurus (and Libra, but we won't go there right now); and when she is in your paddock, she comes on as Venus as in Aphrodite, the Greek goddess of having it all, regardless of who it belongs to. She was unstoppable when pursuing handsome mortals, golden apples, or whatever else she desired. You've got a big hitter on your side; be grateful. Astrological logistics (*see pages 8–9*) mean that your Venus will be in Taurus, Pisces, Aries, Gemini, or Cancer.

Hot Taurus Role Models

James Brown, May 3, 1933
The hardest-working man in showbiz, self-styled sex machine, and creator of super-heavy funk. Got on up for over half a century, showing the kind of relentless stamina that only Taurus can produce.

Audrey Hepburn, May 4, 1929
a.k.a. Holly Golightly. Breakfast at Tiffany's? Waffles, champagne, diamonds *and* pearls? Could life get any more stuffed with what Taurus likes best?

Venus in Taurus

Venus in Taurus, when you're already Taurus, is just a license to stalk. Nothing is going to stop you getting what you want—even if what you want doesn't want you. You herd the target into a corner of a remote field, then shower them with kisses, chocolate, and inappropriate expensive gifts; this is to distract them while you tether them to the spot.

Venus in Pisces

Venus in Pisces is manipulative and changeable, but you're still a bull, so you express this via needy nuzzling, fluttering your big bovine eyelashes, and lowing piteously until your mark is in too deep to get out. Then you trot off to the next field with their best friend.

Venus in Aries

Venus is Mars's partner, and so when she is in Aries it's a very incandescent date indeed. None of this wearing down your target's defenses just by standing still and looking gorgeous. You put your head down and charge, muscles rippling; they get out of the way or you bowl them over. You don't mind either way.

Venus in Gemini

This placing means you are a tiny bit more sprightly on your hooves in the sexual arena than other bulls. Sometimes you'll take a date somewhere you've been to only once before, and some of you even change your pickup line every couple of years.

Venus in Cancer

Scary: Aphrodite and smother-mom all in one package. On hot dates, you pack Band-Aids® and a spare comforter, and home-baked cakes are your aphrodisiac of choice. If the date doesn't work out, you can always bring them home and eat them yourself.

Gemini

May 21–June 20

Want to have the pants charmed off you and then sold on eBay? Longing to meet someone really sincere, who can spend your own money in a much more stylish manner than you could even dream of? Happy to be one of a crowd and to have the wool pulled over your eyes? Fascinating, smooth-tongued multitasker with charisma to spare and a high plausibility rating WLTM anybody with prospects; age and looks not an issue—I'm much more interested in your hidden assets. Give me a call anytime day or night, but especially night. What have you got to lose?

One-night stand

Your favorite. There's a book running in the zodiac somewhere covering the bets made between Geminis on how long it will take you to get from "Well, hi there" to home plate, and how many you can do in one night; you get great odds on doing a . double or triple jump.

Two-year stretch

Not your top choice, because it means death by boredom. If forced (maybe you made an overambitious bet), you inject some sport into the mix by trying out wilder and wilder excuses for your nights away and by awarding points for how many times you talk your partner around.

Long-haul

The received wisdom is: dear God, no—but you did not get where you are today without lateral thinking; this could be quite fun if you go for the parallel worlds option. Set everyone up in different states, tell them you are an astronaut/pilot/trucker/sailor/spy, then visit when it suits you.

Gemini in Love
what's love got to do with it?

Oh, get real. Love requires putting someone else first in your life. As if! And apparently you're supposed to open up your heart and soul and share your innermost secrets. How dumb would you have to be? And let's not get you started on intimate evenings alone with just you two and the beloved to flirt with. Of course, as the zodiac's top grifter and mimic, you put on a great show—melting eye contact, subtle knee stroking, enigmatic sighing, clever *haikus* about the slant of the beloved's cheek, etc.—and fool quite a lot of the people quite a lot of the time, but it's just lust you're in, not love. You know this, of course, but if you told your lovers, they might believe you and not come across. Why risk it?

Stalker?

Why waste your time; once you have been there and done that, you move on. There's plenty more Pisceans in the sea.

Tease?

Promise them everything, tell them anything, take what you want, and leave before they see what you've done.

Gold digger?

If lovers fall over themselves to hand you power of attorney, another Rolex, the keys to the safe, etc., what can you do?

Twin pickup lines

The maestro of the sure-fire line; you've probably got a publishing deal.
♥ I'm doing a survey: what's the worst pickup line you've ever heard?
♥ Which end of the bath do you prefer?
♥ Hi

Dating Gemini

round, round, get around

It's all in the wrist; the trick is to cast a wide net, so you get a varied catch; your special skill is to keep them all alive and deliciously wriggling while you take your pick. You are such a broad-spectrum flirt that there is no chance you won't get a date, and probably two or three on the same night. Thank Mercury for Bluetooth®, you cry, as you juggle your cell with your BlackBerry®, coordinating restaurant bookings with show times.

All of your dates must bring a big fat wallet or preloaded plastic, because one of your favorite gambits is "I was mugged on the way here and they took my Black Card and the keys to my Lexus"; this line, plus a few brave winces and a bit of fake blood for window dressing, guarantees a free dinner and a mercy lay. As for speed-dating, why pay for doing what comes naturally? You should sue Rabbi Deyo for intellectual piracy.

If the rest of the zodiac want to bag a Gemini, they should just hang around in bars, casinos, and racetracks in the afternoon and look available; you will find them. Body language is one of your native tongues—all those little tells, so useful at your poker sessions, pay out big time in the dating game.

You like to bedazzle and show off, so you take them to a foreign movie or an edgy badboy's bar or cross-dressing cabaret (you're always a bit blurred about gender), or to tango classes—anywhere with other people to flirt with over your date's shoulder. You rarely have to hold out for a third date, and always go back to their place, because either you're already married or you haven't made this month's rent and are sleeping on a friend's couch. Will you call again? Just often enough to keep them interested. Who knows when you might need a bed for the night?

Romance Levels

— incandescent

— burning

— hot

— warm

— cool

— cold

— sub-zero

Gemini love token

You never actually buy anything, but like to be memorably fascinating, so if they're loaded, you give them the Homer Simpson key ring you got free with your Happy Meal™; and if they're dirt poor, you give them a Bulgari borrowed from your Taurus roomie (you can palm it back later). It's the thought that counts.

Gemini online

Using your scammed AirPort card, you piggyback on the upstairs apartment's wireless to service your online addiction; you were an early adopter of this risk-free way to expand your daterbase (geddit?). Now you've got so many avatars, passwords, and profiles that you have been forced to flirt big time with an Aquarian geek long enough for them to build you a personal search engine so that you can find your way around your own conquests. Of course you've got a website: www. piedpiper.com.

What gets Gemini hot

Where shall I start? You can have sexual fantasies while you are actually acting out a sexual fantasy. While filming your partner making out with your best friend, you fantasize about a group scene with an actual group: local fire squad, the Chicago Symphony Orchestra, the Knicks. The threat of getting caught is also a bit of a thrill, so you like to do it in the last subway car, under the boardroom table, in church, etc.

Between the sheets

You have to stay versatile to please the crowd, so you don't have a favorite position; it's more fun to surprise your partners and yourself. There's nothing you can't or won't do, except maybe lay still. Anything in motion with a built-in exit strategy is fine by you—up and down the stairs, on a trapeze, hanging from the chandelier. You favor positions where you face forward, as you can get away quickly, plus you are already facing forward, scanning for the next delicious piece that wanders past.

Sex with Gemini

game theory

Not for you long, languorous nights between satin sheets with just the one lover. Your sex drive is coupled to your head, not your heart. It's all a game to you—singles, mixed doubles, five-a-side, World Series—and you are a pro who likes to move up the league. If there's no excited crowd or adrenaline surge, you just don't want to come, which is why you are a founding member of the Mile High Club, the K2 It's Great on Top Collective, and the Mariana Trench Going Down Slow Society. If you've failed to blag air tickets to anywhere exotically erotic, you're adaptable—you can make do with a good ol' All-American orgy with just a couple of dozen buddies of all genders and a vat of mayo. If some of the guys don't show, you can always improvise with some cross-dressing role-play; who doesn't love a pirate in eyeliner?

Gemini and Mars

As you have seen (*see page 9*), Mars is the planet of assertiveness, and wherever it is jogging on the spot in your birthchart decides whether you are just all talk or prepared to put other parts of you where your mouth is. If your Mars is in Gemini, as well as your Sun, it makes you reckless and physical as well as inventive and experimental, so you are often found doing it in the road—probably the New Jersey Turnpike.

Gemini sex toys

The full toy box: glove puppets, celeb masks, marker pens for improvised body poetry, jump ropes; and you always pack a pocket-sized double-ended vibrator. You never know.

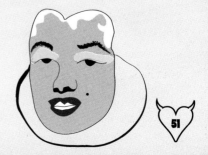

Incompatibility Charts

gemini vs. the rest

Brightsiders say that Gemini (masculine, Air, mutable, compulsive liar) gets along best with other Air signs who'll understand (Libra and Aquarius), and worst with Virgo, Sagittarius, and Pisces (the other mutable signs who think fickle is good). However, this is the Darkside, where everybody is incompatible with everyone else. Here's how.

Gemini and Aries Dump you before you dump them—a salutary swig of your own medicine, but without the sweet aftertaste you always leave. You stay friends; a bit of muscle is always useful.

Gemini and Taurus You are bored rigid at their first hello, but they are such a joy to string along, and the food is so great, that you hang around far too long, lose your edge, and wake up married.

Gemini and Gemini What a coincidence that you are both temporarily impoverished trustafarians looking for love in a cruel world. How silly do you both look when the checks bounce.

Gemini and Cancer Look, you're doing them a favor. They love being loved and left, and treated like a used gourd. Why should you feel any remorse or guilt? It's what they would have wanted.

Gemini and Leo This one's a pushover; tell them you're gonna make them a star, and they'll roll over and purr. When the diva tantrums get tedious, just clear the bank account and skip town.

Gemini and Virgo Not only another mutable sign, but also shares your ruler, Mercury. This means they will smother your every betrayal with understanding and forgiveness. There's no way out.

Gemini and Libra A cardinal Air sign, so more focused than you on how to get something for nothing; you won't win this one, but stick around to get a free masterclass in Practical Flirting.

Gemini and Scorpio This is not for you. All your elaborate excuses and betrayals wither in the glare of their black gaze, and you start blabbing about stuff you haven't even done yet.

Gemini and Sagittarius Another mutable, and your opposite sign, but a glorious pairing, you could be Butch and Sundance. You almost regret skipping town and leaving them to take the rap.

Gemini and Capricorn Step out of your comfort zone and snap up the chance to lead the zodiac's Mr. Repression astray; it will be hard work (yuk!), but think of the fat alimony.

Gemini and Aquarius Another Air sign like you, but with more sticking power, so sees through your every lie and bamboozles you by only ever telling the truth. You can't handle that.

Gemini and Pisces The last mutable sign, much more deeply devious than you. They'll never break your heart, but their silky emotional blackmail skills will put a severe dent in your professional pride.

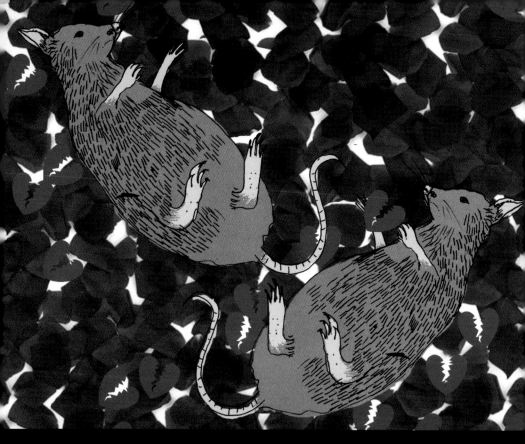

Love rat?

Smart rat: however many you have on the go, you manage to keep them all sweet, because it's only sensible to keep the granaries full and to ensure you have a warm welcome in every port. If it's time for a cull, you behave really atrociously and hope that some of them still have enough shreds of dignity left to dump you. Then you can act shattered and sorrowful, and guilt them into handing over half the condo.

GETTING BACK AT GEMINI

Memo to rest of zodiac (except Scorpio): Gemini is way too smart to let you get back at them—they wrote the manual on this kind of thing. Taking the SIM cards from all their cells would slow them down a bit, but it may be better just to walk away and picture them thwarted and lonely in old age.

Your Cheatiŋ' Heart
doing what comes naturally

You can't resist chasing besotted frogs. Can you help it if they turn into dull, handsome princes when you kiss them, and have to be thrown back in the pond? It's kinder in the long run. It's not your fault; you suffer from CFS (Congenital Flirt Syndrome); you're constantly looking over the shoulder of whoever you are currently bewitching, radar on high alert for anyone cuter, richer, more famous, or more likely to get you that job. The words "relationship" and "permanent" go together like peaches and plutonium in your book. Your idea of commitment is to restrict yourself to three or four concurrent partners and cheat on all of them all at once—but only once a week. You can tell them you are a wanderer, etc., but no one listens because everyone wants to be the one who nails you down.

Gemini excuses

"I'm so sorry I missed your birthday, but my old college roomie needs a new kidney; I'm not compatible, but I just had to spend last week being tested." Masterly! Shows you as selfless and sincere and makes complaining look cheap. We are not worthy.

Gemini pre-nup

This is drawn up by a fellow Gemini paralegal, and will look very impressive, with lots of ribbon, Latin, and sealing wax. The tiny print gives you indemnity against any legal action brought against you for fraud, aggravated lying, breach of contract, neglect, fire, and theft, while committing you to nothing. If they look carefully, they will see that you have signed it George Washington.

Venus and Gemini

sweet-talking guy

Mercury (your ruler) blarneyed the goddess of love into bed, even though he was:
a) her half brother, and b) only the courier; that's what happens when a silver tongue
meets a gold-standard flirt. When you two come together you make an irresistibly
seductive pairing, and leave a trail of broken hearts and rosy memories all over the
zodiac—even when Venus is off playing coy in other signs. Astrological logistics
(*see pages 8–9*) mean that your Venus will be in Gemini, Aries, Taurus, Cancer, or Leo.

Hot Gemini Role Models

Marilyn Monroe, June 1, 1926
Still blazing in the world's collective libido
as the sexiest women on Earth, despite
being dead for 45 years. Who wouldn't
want to be loved by Norma-Jeane?

Marquis de Sade, June 2, 1740
Not only an Olympic-class sexual athlete
with an -ism all his own, but also wrote
down his every fantasy, which is how
we know all about him. There's no point
being hot stuff if you don't tell anyone.

Venus in Gemini

Venus in Gemini, when you are already Gemini, means that you are the *sensei* of the Flirting Dojo, with a 4th Dan black belt. When you suspect that your four fiancé(e)s, five spouses and 39 live-in lovers are beginning to wonder if they are not alone in the kingdom of your heart, you pour on the silky-smooth sweet talk and truck in bulk-bought love tokens to soothe them.

Venus in Aries

Venus in Aries means that she is back with her old boyfriend (Mars), which just makes you competitive and determined to win. You put your band of lovers through erotic boot camp so that they can be the best. Sex games tend to involve a lot of collateral damage.

Venus in Taurus

Venus rules Taurus, so you feel pretty sure of yourself because you have plenty of solid backup. You've got a whole treeful of love nests that you won in a dubious crap game. You like to line them with almost undetectably forged bank notes and some knock-off Cartier to attract the unwary.

Venus in Cancer

Not only do you love them like a mom (let's not go there), you talk to them like a mom as well. So you lash them to their beds with your apron strings and, just as they're thinking "yo, milf!", you start gettin' tetchy on them because they didn't eat your homebaked brownie.

Venus in Leo

You are already married (for dynastic reasons), but as a royal you are free to lead your own love life. You like to have new lovers sent in by the batch, as tributes from smaller kingdoms. If you like any of them, you might marry them as well. Monogamy is for little people.

Cancer

June 21–July 20

Gorgeous, smart, talented, loaded A-lister sought as way-out-of-league love object for moody, angst-ridden, Z-list grump to pine pointlessly over. Secretly, WLTM someone to share life's downside and be there for me during the bad times; if you like howling at the moon, undifferentiated worrying, and counting your grudges, you'd be perfect—so I wouldn't want to meet you, because I just know it would all go wrong. I don't suppose anyone will reply to this, but if you do, don't leave a message, because I won't get back to you. PS: My mom made me place this ad; she says I have to move out.

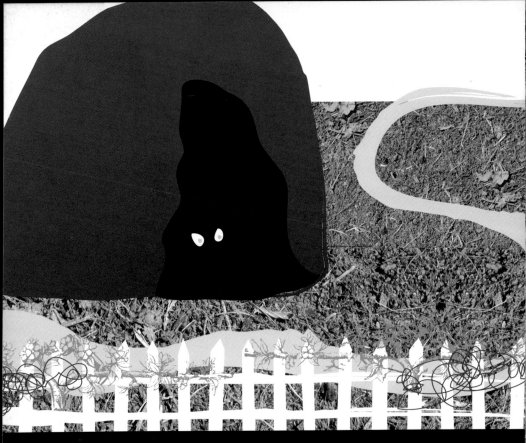

One-night stand

This sometimes happens to you because, in the grand scheme of things, it's quicker to say yes to a persistent date and get it over with than deal with the sexual jousting that other signs seem so hooked on. They are going to leave you anyway, so why not cut the waiting time?

Two-year stretch

It always takes you about two years to feel cautiously confident enough to tell your partner that you think you might make a go of it. Ironically, this is just the same time it takes for them to conclude that you don't give a damn and to wriggle free from your clawlike grip.

Long-haul

Hell, yes! You don't like to let anyone go, so this is just your poisoned chalice. It doesn't have to be a happy and productive union; it's much better if it isn't, otherwise you will have nothing to moan and whinge about, and the entire C & W music industry would disappear overnight.

Cancer in Love

love hurts

Crabs are always in love; it's just that no one can tell (not even the loved one). If there isn't a lover hidden in your great pincer, you are pining inside for someone totally unreachable (married, famous, fictional, dead). Unreciprocated love is best, because it offers superior martyring opportunities and will never let you down. The trouble with loving anybody real and available, who just might love you back, is that you are constantly fretting about when they are going to discover the real you and leave. To make it easier for them to go, you come on like their spare mom/dad, spike their mojitos with vitamins, disapprove of their friends, call the office to check they got in safely, and feed them apple pie until they pop an artery.

Stalker?

No. You spend your time scuttling sideways away from the love object, in case they notice you and make you talk.

Tease?

No, but your natural, hard-to-get default mode is often mistaken for teasing, and you get unfairly bad-mouthed.

Gold digger?

No, but you are always charitable toward the old and plain; is it your fault they turn out to be eccentric billionaires?

Crab pickup lines

You don't have pickup lines. Who'd want to talk to you? Instead you:
- ♥ Stand next to the one you want and ignore them pointedly
- ♥ Go into another room
- ♥ Leave

Datıŋg Caŋçer

hard to get

Dating Cancer is a nonstarter anyway because of your inoperable Groucho complex; you never want to date the kind of people who would want to date someone like you. In brief interludes of remission, when you see someone you like, your strategy is to leave the country or sit very still, pincer on stun, and wait for them to make the first move. The theory is that, struck by your moody mystery (who is this fascinating moonlit enigma?), the chosen one will pursue you. It's a form of quality control: if they really, really want you, they won't mind hacking through the defensive brambles and pokeweed to get to your secret inner loveliness. If it doesn't happen, you would rather dance alone in the dark.

Speed-dating won't help, because it's your idea of hell. It's bad enough having to talk about yourself for two whole minutes to one person, let alone 30.

If other signs really want to date you, they will find you in dark corners or in the kitchen at parties. If you do actually get a date, you are always late (you don't believe they will turn up and don't want to look pathetically eager). You go to dark movie theaters, smallish art galleries, indie bookshops, or the seashore—anyplace you can stand/sit side by side and look at something together, without having to speak to one another. If your date is with a fellow Crab, it will be long and silent as you wait for each other to initiate conversation.

If you get to a third date and haven't yet scuttled away, you always go to their place because you don't want them to know where you live—and anyway yours is a mess and covered in cat hairs. Will you call again? Of course not, but you will sit at home waiting for them to call you, so that you can hang up on them.

Romance Levels

- incandescent
- burning
- hot
- warm
- cool
- cold
- sub-zero

Cancer love token

This will be your favorite childhood teddy bear. Basically, you're scent-marking. When it all goes wrong, you get to sob and pine over your loss, and they are stuck with a permanent reminder of you—unless they are icy-hearted enough to throw Teddy in the Goodwill box. Second choice is a tray of homebaked cupcakes.

Cancer online

Crab heaven! Sit safely at home in your own mess, with comfort food and soothing tunes, and search the Web for love, confident that if you find that special someone, there's no danger of ever having to meet them face-to-face. Live chatrooms are not you—they're nearly as nerve-racking as real-time talking—but dating sites, where you get to see all the candidates and they can't see you, satisfy the picky, lookist voyeur that lurks behind your beady little glare. You're too scared to post your own photo.

63

What gets Cancer hot

Because being needed is what really turns you on, one of your major fantasies is the wounded lover who cannot escape your caring clutch; they must have attractive scars and bruising, plus a minor injury that confines them to bed, but loads of stamina, because you intend to heal them by having hours of nonstop, well-lubricated sex during which you will not be able to tell whether they are groaning in agony or moaning with

Between the sheets

Mostly missionary: it's traditional, comfy, accommodates awkward shapes and you can control things secretly from underneath (where you like to be, so if anyone bursts in, you can hide); plus the association with martyrdom adds a frisson. Across the kitchen table is favorite, so you can keep an eye on your soufflé. Otherwise sideways—nestled like spoons in a picnic basket or just side by side lying on the beach at midnight staring

Sex with Cancer

protected sex

At first glance, sex with an armored personnel carrier is not much of a turn-on (except for Aries, who gets hot over anything military). Foreplay consists of winkling you out of your shell—a long, tedious process, which doubles as a natural wastage system for lightweights. This is a cunning plan: you have noticed in your shrewd, beady little way that deferred gratification is the way to keep people hanging on, so that you can hang on to them, which is the object of your every exercise. Life's not quite long enough for tantric sex, as far as you're concerned, and you can go so-o-o slow that many lovers (especially those with a job, life, etc.) give up/fall asleep/leave you to get on with it alone. Also, moving too fast gives you unsightly shell-burn, and you're not wieldy enough for bendy *Kama Sutra*-style action or anything that involves chandeliers.

Cancer and Mars

As you know (*see page 9*), Mars is the planet of going forward; where it moves (or just sits) in your birthchart determines whether you are passive, aggressive, or both together. You are the sign of going sideways, which changes the Martian angle of approach, and if your Mars is in Cancer, as well as your Sun, then you are at once assertive and emotional, so while you like hot, intense sex, it sure as hell better not be meaningless.

Cancer sex toys

Too embarrassing—and crabs aren't flexible enough for role-play. Velvet apron strings to hold your lover down? A cat (by default)? Mascarpone and a spatula (you need the calcium for your shell)?

65

Incompatibility Charts
cancer vs. the rest

Brightsiders say that Cancer (feminine, Water, cardinal, passive-aggressive) gets along best with other Water signs who'll understand (Scorpio and Pisces), and worst with Libra, Capricorn, and Aries (the other cardinal signs who like it on top). However, this is the Darkside, where everybody is incompatible with everyone else. Here's how.

Cancer and Aries Anything armored (like you) is a magnet to them, and they are a fellow cardinal sign so want to show who's boss. Sit it out in your shell until they run out of steam.

Cancer and Taurus You never let go, and neither do they, so although you are totally mismatched and fight constantly in the kitchen, it will take a team of stunt divorce lawyers to pry you apart.

Cancer and Gemini You love it when they don't turn up and you wait lonely and foolish in a downtown bar for the call they won't make; they're your main angst dealer, you'll never quit them.

Cancer and Cancer Disastrous. A crab-on-crab relationship is always full of long, moody, uncomfortable silences that only end when one of you dies—and maybe not even then.

Cancer and Leo A winner. You are happy to be Moon to their Sun, and scuttle along behind them bathed in reflected glory; it's even better if they are involved with someone else.

Cancer and Virgo It was all fine until the third date back at your place, where they blew out the candles (fire risk!), emptied the bubble bath (parabens!), and ran a cold shower for you both instead.

Cancer and Libra Another cardinal sign, so a possible trap. You can feel yourself being managed, got around, and charmed out of your foul moods, and that makes you as mad as hell.

Cancer and Scorpio A fellow Water sign, so you have a bond, but they have no power over you, because they'll never be able to make you feel more deliciously wretched than you can yourself.

Cancer and Sagittarius When they appear at your window, a pair of air tickets to Rio between their teeth, and say, "Let's elope," you push the ladder away. It would never have worked out.

Cancer and Capricorn The last cardinal sign, so probably only with you so that they can stand on your shell to boost themselves higher up the social ladder. Why else would anybody want you?

Cancer and Aquarius How can you relate to someone who spoils your entire worldview by explaining how your melancholia is just a matter of light levels, seratonins, and brain chemistry?

Cancer and Pisces The last Water sign and your nemesis; Pisces pulls at every emotional string to get you to be their mom, lover, piggy bank, and defense lawyer. You can't resist.

67

Love rat?

The opposite. Love ratting would be harsher, but quicker. You clamp your great pincer to the relationship and cling on. When love is dying, you don't mourn and move on; you hook your pincer to the life-support system and hang around the deathbed being caring. Ex-partners have to emigrate, marry someone else, join a closed religious order, or die before you will accept that it's over; even then you demand to see the death certificate.

GETTING BACK AT CANCER

It's so easy to devastate a Crab that the more sporting signs don't bother. If you really want to pierce their shell, tell their local realtor that they want to put their apartment on the market, or send that clip of them looking fat and dumb into *America's Funniest Home Videos* for everyone to laugh at.

Your Cheatin' Heart

how can they miss you when you won't go?

Crabs rarely cheat, because you're afraid you'll get caught (with your security protocols? I don't think so) and have to do Confrontation. You'd rather suffer. Think about it: if you are in a relationship (it could happen) and you meet Another, you get an unmissable opportunity for legitimate pining while you stay loyally, to keep the home fires sputtering. This could last a lifetime. It's even better to be Another (higher pining quotient): Crabs of all genders suffer from Mistress Syndrome—the addiction to the aching poignancy of the lonely Christmas tree and the telephone that doesn't ring, the e-mail that doesn't ping. You never dump; you just make yourself grumpier, moodier, and more depressed than usual (how can they tell?) so that your partner (unless it's a fellow Crab) is finally forced to cut their losses and leave. Pining time again!

Cancer excuses

These are always delivered by letter, txt, or e-mail, because you can't do face-to-face (or even mouth-to-ear). Why do people get so pissed when you don't show up to the intimate dinner for two? They only invited you out of pity because no one else on their list could make it.

Cancer pre-nup

You hate legal stuff, but you do like your security, so your unwritten pre-nup is enforced by mom maneuvers such as tight-lipped silence alternating with total recall of wild promises made years before when you were both drunk (although you weren't). Conditions include not reading your diaries, understanding what you mean without you having to say, and never telling you, "Cheer up: it may never happen."

Venus and Cancer
sibling rivalry

Your ruler, the Moon, has its own goddess, Artemis (Diana); up on Mount Olympus she is half sister to Aphrodite (Venus). And you know what a bitchfest that can be, girlfriend. Sometimes you're sharing lip-gloss, at other times you're scratching each other's eyes out. Venus is fickle, the Moon has murderous mood swings, and when you're together it can all get a bit synchronized PMS. Astrological logistics (*see pages 8–9*) mean that your Venus will be in Cancer, Taurus, Gemini, Leo, or Virgo.

Hot Cancer Role Models

Diana, Princess of Wales, July 1, 1961
Named for the goddess of the Moon (and the hunt), the caring people's princess who unerringly found her way to the Darkside of the fairytale.

Ernest Hemingway, July 21, 1899
Tight-lipped, grouchy stoic, known to all as "Papa" and famous for recording the sound of tectonic plate-shifting during hot sex; or maybe it was just his own shell creaking under pressure.

Venus in Cancer

Venus in Cancer, when you are already Cancer, means that you are unstoppably caring. Everybody's deeply moved by your unswerving loyalty and heart-warming devotion—except for your desperate beloved, who has tried every known love-rat maneuver, including marriage and amnesia, and still can't shake you off; the prison guard of love.

Venus in Taurus

This placing gives Venus an extra scoop of possessiveness. You're the love bully on page 3 of the *National Enquirer*, under headlines like "Spurned Lover Slays Partner and Self in Remote Love Nest" (via a unilateral suicide pact involving poisoned muffins). Nobody leaves you unless you say so.

Venus in Gemini

In this position, Venus makes you a little less beady-eyed. You may even pimp your shell (even though it will all wash off next time the tide comes in). You might even clamber out of it and go for a little cautious flirting in the dark; you can jump back in at the first sign of love danger.

Venus in Leo

Venus here gives you grandiose ideas above your station, so you morph into King Crab, lurk behind the rocks, and spring on your unsuspecting prey. You knock them senseless with your great big masterful claw, then take them home to your palace by the ocean.

Venus in Virgo

When Venus is in Virgo, all that lust energy has to get sublimated somewhere, and in your case it goes into self-interested do-goodery. You cruise the beach looking for the inadequate, lure them in with herbal tea and sympathy, and snag yourself a live-in punching bag who owes you a living.

Leo

July 21–August 22

Are you good enough? Fantastic opportunity to upgrade your love and sex life (unexpectedly available owing to ridiculous booking fubar by ex-management). Me: handsome, gorgeous, successful, clever, übertalented, top-of-the-range alpha golden overachiever. You: beautiful, but not quite as beautiful as me, well dressed, rich, and grateful. If you give great grovel and are connected (Hollywood, rock aristocracy, minor European royalty, Donald Trump, Oprah, *Vogue*, the Clintons), get in touch now and my people will get back to you as soon as they have vetted your photograph.

One-night stand

This is part of your outreach program. It's your royal duty to take an interest in as many of the little people as you can, and what better way than to get down on the streets in disguise, to find out if they all love you as they should? Anyway, working's better than waiting tables.

Two-year stretch

You'd like a longer run, but this is as much as anyone can take of your flouncing, playing away, showing off, chronic vacation habit, crowd-pleasing, Versace addiction, and making time for everyone else but them. It makes you cry, but not enough to blotch your face.

Long-haul

Who turns down the lead in a long-running box-office cert? Or a favorable alliance to secure the throne? You can always go out nights for some *droit de seigneur* action, can't you, or call in an understudy and indulge yourself in a little indie movie or an off-off-off-Broadway piece?

Leo in Love
all the world's a stage

What is love, if not a chance to stand center stage in a pool of flattering light singing a great aria all about yourself and how much you adore poor but beautiful young whosit, and how the cruel world must shift to make room for a love that is bigger than both of you? Leo rules the heart, so you always appear to be in love (especially with yourself); this is partly because everybody apparently loves a lover, and you need everybody to love you at all times, but mainly because you are the zodiac's thespian and adore making grand theatrical gestures, like swearing to swim the seven seas, climb the highest mountain, leap through fiery hoops, die, etc. Note that you never promise to take out the trash or get a real job.

Stalker?

You're a lion, so stalking is a hard-wired behavior trait; but it's all over after the pounce and the killing bite.

Tease?

You'll promise to do whatever it takes to get the gig, but will reserve the royal prerogative to change your mind.

Gold digger?

So what's wrong with an alliance where you bring the handsomeness and chutzpah and they bring the money?

Lion pickup lines

Corny as Kansas in August, but always delivered with a swagger:
- 💜 Why don'tcha come up some time, and see me?
- 💜 You just got lucky
- 💜 I can get you a backstage pass

Dating Leo

group therapy

Without dating, you would die, because you need megatons of adoration to stay alive. Even you realize that no individual human can grind out quite as much unconditional attention as you demand, so do your best to spread the load. Your usual prey are trustafarians, models, White House interns, etc., but you also have a weakness for downmarket cuteness and like to patronize cocktail waitresses or busboys because they are so grateful.

You went speed-dating for a laugh, but rather missed the point as you leaped onto the table in the middle of the room and did your spiel to all 30 datees at once. You can't resist a captive audience; anyway, 15 of them checked your box.

As long as they are cute enough, and can fawn, any sign can audition for a date with Leo; you are very high profile and can always be found at hot-ticket gatherings, pre-Oscar-night drinkfests, wrap parties, openings of envelopes, etc., radiating charm and loveliness. If they get the part, you take them to watch you play in your Kings of Leon tribute band, act your socks off as Brick/Maggie in the amateur production of *Cat on a Hot Tin Roof* that you directed, or go to see your exhibition of mixed media self-portraits, and afterward to your favorite restaurant, where you sit at a window table and you order their meal for them and tell them what they thought of the show.

You don't mind waiting for the third date (it gives you more showing-off time) and always take them to your place because it will be way grander than theirs; plus they may not have enough mirrors or lights. If they've been sycophantic enough, of course you'll call back, as soon as you have a slot in your agenda. It never does to upset a fan.

Romance Levels

— incandescent

— burning

— hot

— warm

— cool

— cold

— sub-zero

Leo love token

What else? A signed photograph of you—a miniature, of course, you're not vain—so they can easily carry it around with them everywhere. If things get serious, you'll give them the larger version in a gold frame to hang on their wall, and will pay someone to come around and fix it.

Leo online

Anything that lets more people see you is great by you. That's why you podcast live from your bedroom, and Bluetooth® your cell camera to one of your Web sites so that you can update on the hour. You don't waste time in grubby chatrooms or dating sites; your other two Web sites have dedicated harem pages, where hopefuls can post their photographs and résumés (a modified spam filter drains off the dull and ugly) so you can look at your leisure and get back to them if you're bored.

What gets Leo hot

Being seen. There is no point in turning in an Oscar performance if no one is looking, so you hire a couple of voyeurs with digital camcorders. Not only do you get a good house for the live show, but you also get the chance later on to make out while watching a home video of you making out. God, you're good! Role-play always gets your fur hot, especially the traditional kind where you are spanked by gorgeous bits of trailer trash, because you have been a very naughty Leo.

Between the sheets

As you are lazy and vain, you'll only go for positions that are comfortable and flattering. On top is not a good look if you haven't kept up to date with your chin tucks. Standing upright will also disguise any slight flab. Spoons means you can always show your best side, and fit in as many admirers as you like. And all cats like licking each other. You don't really care as long as there are enough mirrors around for you to check out your action and reflect your glory.

Sex with Leo
darling, I was wonderful

What your lovely assistants have to realize is that Leo sex is all about performance and applause. Just because you're experiencing blinding, intimate, thigh-drenching passion doesn't mean you have to be alone. Anyhow, your definition of intimate is just you, your partners, your hair-and-beauty people, your aromatherapist, your aura cleanser, your fitness coach, the camera crew, your fluffer (just in case), and a few gofers. You take your part seriously, buffing up at the gym, rehearsing the grinds and thrusts with your Pilates guru, but on the night you focus so hard on style, posture, and execution that you fail to notice that your partners have gone to sleep. You throw a huge sulk, because it means they will not be able to give you marks out of 10 with the special numbered cards you have prepared, or offer a round of wild applause and scream for an encore.

Leo and Mars

As we have seen (*see page 9*), Mars is planet Yang; wherever it's strutting in your birthchart dictates just how many cojones you got, and how big they are. You are the Yangest sign of the zodiac, so if your Mars is in Leo as well as your Sun, it's scorched sheets all around; you come on hard and fast, and stay on even harder and faster.

Leo sex toys

They're not toys, they are performance-enhancing props and costume: fishnet stockings, garters, a velvet blindfold, and a stage whip always do it for you.

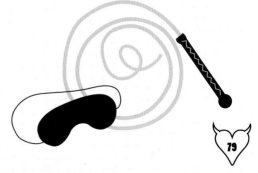

Incompatibility Charts
leo vs. the rest

Brightsiders say that Leo (masculine, Fire, fixed, delusional) gets along best with other Fire signs who'll understand (Sagittarius and Aries), and worst with Scorpio, Aquarius, and Taurus (the other fixed signs whose middle name is obstinacy). However, this is the Darkside, where everybody is incompatible with everyone else. Here's how.

Leo and Aries Another Fire sign, the raging inferno to your stylish source of heat and light. You, above all signs, love to be passionately adored, but when they singed your hair, they had to go.

Leo and Taurus Another fixed sign, so they refuse to adore you publicly as much as you deserve, considering how exciting you make them look. If it wasn't for their Gold Card, you'd sack them.

Leo and Gemini You fall for this one every time; your addiction to gross flattery and mingling with celebs (Gemini always knows everybody) overrides your need to be the only one in their lives.

Leo and Cancer It's great to have a spare mom who will clean up after you, comfort you when others don't appreciate you, and indulge your every whim, but you'd rather not be seen out with them.

Leo and Leo High-wattage celeb partnerships never work: Burton and Taylor, Lopez and Affleck, you and Leo: all doomed because there is not enough room in the spotlight for both of you.

Leo and Virgo I don't think so; they cut your hair, cramp your style, and curb your enthusiasm. And how can you perform your killer Meatloaf karaoke act in an alcohol-free vegan juice bar?

Leo and Libra Ancient kings had favorites, and they were probably all Libran; they give great professional adoration, but don't expect them to stick around if your crown slips.

Leo and Scorpio A fixed sign like you, so you know at gut level there's a power struggle going on, but can't work out why they always come out on top, even though you're much more glorious.

Leo and Sagittarius A fellow Fire sign, but wildfire to your burning hearth; dates with them always end with mussed hair and having to explain to the police chief who you are. Too undignified.

Leo and Capricorn Works well for a bit; they like your social status, you like their gravitas and the way they smell of money. It's less fun when you realize they aren't spending any of it on you.

Leo and Aquarius The last fixed sign and your stubborn opposite; on the first (and last) date they deliberately took you to a back table in a dark, damp cellar bar where no one could see you.

Leo and Pisces You pick them out of the entourage because they look meek and pliable and you love to patronize trailer trash. They repay you by telling Oprah what a wild beast you are in bed.

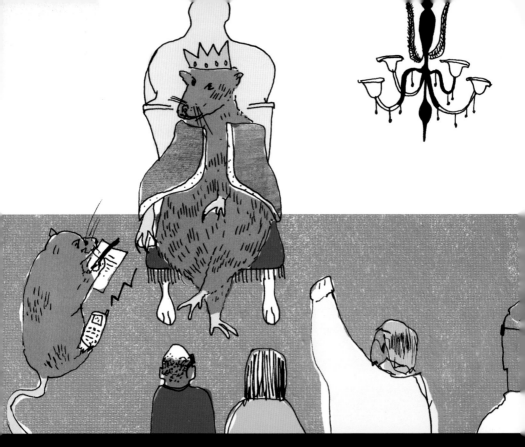

Love rat?

Once the thrill has gone and your ardor has cooled, you simply can't be bothered to tell your ex that they are an ex; if they get tiresome and keep calling, you may get one of your people to text them, or put out a press release in *US* magazine. Exile will do them good and keep them keen; when you let them back into the charmed circle, they'll work twice as hard to please you and will up the groveling.

GETTING BACK AT LEO

Play on their snobbery, vanity, and limelight fixation. It will cost, but they're worth it. Pay a team of paps to mob their dim neighbor and ignore them; turn up as their banjo-dueling cousin when they cohost a charity lunch with Anna Wintour; book up their hairdresser for the next year.

Your Cheatin' Heart

leo rules

Heads will roll if people don't quit going on about how you are married to someone else and somehow that's a problem. You didn't actually mean to be married; this was way back when you were young, before you'd perfected the Idyllic-Wedding-Ceremony-on-Caribbean-Island-with-No-Binding-Legal-Status strategy—but you are. Of course it doesn't slow you down; you are so gorgeous that it's practically a Darwinian imperative that you put yourself about.

You made the rules of this little game, so it's technically impossible for you to cheat. If your lover stops laughing at your jokes, gets an unflattering haircut, criticizes anything you do, takes a job in Wal-Mart, or disagrees with your movie choice, you can invoke rule 406 and dump them without warning. Don't be silly; no one would ever dump you.

Leo excuses

Enter Leo, mad as hell: "How could you possibly even think that I would do such a thing? [*Strides up and down, waving arms.*] "I'm deeply—no, mortally—wounded." [*Almost in tears now.*] "If you can't trust me, it's all over!" *Sweeping gesture. Dramatic exit. Applause. Oscar.*

Leo pre-nup

Great! You love a royal charter. Can it be in gold ink? You may be divalicious, but you are extremely shrewd, so all the money stuff is in very tiny type right at the bottom. Much more important are the clauses specifying the number of hours per day to be spent focusing undivided attention on you; how many gifts you should get per hour; and the guarantee of your immunity from ever being wrong.

83

Venus and Leo

solar eclipse

The Sun (your ruler, naturally) is the star of our local solar system, pumping out Yang and thrust and all-around alphadom: the top jock to Venus's prom queen. When you two are together, you make the rest of the zodiac feel kind of resentful, ugly, lumpy, and dressed wrong; you are the golden couple who reign over the charmed circle we just know we're never going to hang out with. Astrological logistics (*see pages 8–9*) means that your Venus will be in Leo, Gemini, Cancer, Virgo, or Libra.

Hot Leo Role Models

Napoleon Bonaparte, August 15, 1769
A triumph of self-belief; from zero to emperor in 35 years, and just as famous as a hot, passionate lover; nothing beats striding straight from battlefield to bed.

Mae West, August 17, 1893
Brash silver-screen goddess who rewrote film scripts to give herself bigger, more scene-stealing parts, cherry-picked her own leading young hunks, and made a career out of sex and showing off.

Venus in Leo

Venus in Leo, when you are already Leo, means that you are extra imperious, demanding, expensive, and impossible. You'd think this would put people off, but the zodiac is stuffed with deluded, weak-willed, servile submissives who can't wait to get in line to be personally pussy-whipped. You'll only oblige if they are powerful, important, rich, and make you look good.

Venus in Gemini

When Venus is on maximum flirt, as here, she sweet-talks you into dropping the dignity and accessing your Inner Kitten. You look so fluffy and adorable that handsome rivals duel to the death to be allowed to stroke your gorgeous fur.

Venus in Cancer

This is the Doting Mom placement, and makes you a very caring royal. You keep all your loves in a gilded cage and stuffed with full-fat, homemade birdseed so that they never rise from the perch. Just to make sure, you clip their wings with your golden scissors.

Venus in Virgo

Venus here means that—regardless of whatever gender—you are the Virgin Queen: hypercritical, unpleasable, and with unlimited powers. No one is good enough for you; reckless chancers who become your short-lived favorites die by a thousand cuts of your sharp tongue.

Venus in Libra

Venus is in one of her own signs here, and so a bit more foot stamping and a lot less coy and complaisant. This is a high-wattage celeb union, all air kissing and backstabbing, shameless upstagery in the intimate love scenes, to-the-death fights over who gets top billing, and custody squabbles over the mirrors.

Virgo

August 23–September 22

Last Tuesday, 4.38 p.m., at the Howard Hughes Allergy Drop-in Center; you: tall, thin, big butt, handwoven poncho, virgin goat's-wool socks, lactose-intolerant; me: tall, thin, virgin goat's-wool socks, incipient wheat problem, marginal OCD. We shared stain-removing tips and sneered at the literals in the Fat-Free Feast recipe leaflet, and you showed me your rash. Let's meet up for a tofu shake (Dutch treat, bring your own recycled glass, you can't be too careful). PS: clean your teeth thoroughly before you come, I noticed some unsightly tartar when you smiled.

One-night stand

This is about all the action that you get, because the rest of the zodiac can't handle more than one evening of your control-freakery. The upside is you're a safe one-nighter because you always glove up and insist on a Clorox® jacuzzi afterward (or even during).

Two-year stretch

This is what happens when you give love a whirl. You go into full makeover mode, changing their diet, clothes, friends, job, apartment, etc. to suit your perfectionist standards. Just when you've got them into shape, they bust out of the cage, and run away screaming.

Long-haul

A lint picker's dream: a live-in punching bag, someone to put down, criticize, and carp about until death do you part; long evenings around an unlit fire telling them just how unsatisfactory they are. Bliss! It usually stays a dream because no one else is that dumb.

Virgo in Love
control yourself

From what you've heard and seen about love, it's a messy old business, and we all know how you feel about mess. People in love are out of control—a concept so disturbing that you have to mainline Rescue™ Remedy even to think about it. How can you possibly act as if every little thing someone else does is magic, when your inner Mr. Fussy knows that it isn't and will explode if you don't tell them exactly where they're going wrong and how to do it better? And what's all this about not having to say you're sorry? The likelihood of you finding anyone (apart from a blow-up doll) who will do things exactly the way you do them is so remote that you will never be swept away by a grand passion. Thank God for that!

Stalker?

You're only checking on that rash, and to make sure they have changed their underwear. A restraining order is OTT.

Tease?

No. You always deliver precisely what you promise, and demand a countersignature in blood (and triplicate) for your records.

Gold digger?

No—you only open their credit card statements to make sure they are running their finances in a sensible manner.

Virgin pickup lines

Telling it like it is always works for you:
- ♥ You've got spinach stuck between your teeth
- ♥ Don't touch the champagne, it's nonorganic
- ♥ Is that pinkeye?

89

Dating Virgo
it's all in the detail

Is there anyone good enough for you out there? Probably not; just as well, really—if there were, you'd have nothing to be picky about. You do well with submissives, who pay money to be looked at like they're roadkill and told they're not worthy to lick your bootstraps, but there just aren't that many around. Speed-dating sounds very efficient (it's a kind of stock-breeding program after all), but when you go, you annoy everyone by querying the quality and quantity of the sample group and by imposing your own far more complex checkbox system.

If anyone is feeling masochistic enough for the Virgo experience, they can find you at multiple pileups telling the paramedics what to do, in the local ayurvedic spa disputing the organic provenance of the seaweed body wrap, or at the Public Records Office exerting your data-mining rights under the Freedom of Information Act. You e-mail the evening's timetable to your date 24 hours in advance, then take them to an early supper at a vegan hotspot, where you change their order for them, insist that they chew each mouthful for 45 seconds, and spend 30 minutes splitting the check scrupulously. (You'd rather bring your own chickpea sandwiches, but you are trying to impress.) Then you get out your laptop for some hardcore data merging over the decaf.

It's a blessing you never get to the third date. Where would you go? If you take them to your place, they may try to use your toothpaste, and anyway you'll have to call in CTS Decon afterward (bodily fluid is a biohazard); if you go to theirs, you will have to spend three days in detox and throw away all your clothes. You wouldn't call back because they would not have been good enough.

Romance Levels

- incandescent
- burning
- hot
- warm
- cool
- cold
- sub-zero

Virgo love token

An electronic organizer, preprogrammed by you. It's patched into your mainframe so that you can give them regular updates (and see their every keystroke). It includes a dictionary so that when you have a lover's tiff about how to spell amebic dysentery, you can prove you're right.

Virgo online

At last! A hygienic remote-control method of intercourse, which takes you out of the nasty germ-ridden social arena and into nice, hyperclean cyberspace. There are long, detailed forms to fill in and you can get as demanding, specific, and micro-managerial as you want and can devise new ways to file and cross-reference your parameters; you don't care that you get few responses (mainly from other Virgos). And as you love to see others degraded, you spend a lot of time policing porn sites.

91

What gets Virgo hot

An astronaut just in from the sterility of space, and shrink-wrapped in Saran™ would really do it for you, but so does getting naked and giving your place a thorough workout with a Dyson. Anyone in scrubs is onto a sure thing, especially if they get in the shower with you and your six-pack of Comet. And there's something about dressing in a firm-control rubber all-in-one and beating people for their own good that always gives you a warm, healthy glow.

Between the sheets

You try to avoid close face-to-face positions as slobbery full-frontal kissing is a bit gross (can you ever be sure that they've flossed properly?). Sitting on top puts you in control, and gives good face-to-face nag time, when you can bring up all their little faults, and they can only squirm. As a back-up, in case your partner ever contradicts you, you have your own annotated copy of the *Kama Sutra* (in wipeclean covers) with amendments where the instructions are not quite clear enough.

Sex with Virgo

health and efficiency

You'd think that all that squidgy bodily-fluid exchange would put you off, but you are an Earth sign, and you know that regular sex is an excellent whole-body workout that supports the circulatory system and relieves stress. You have your black Neoprene all-in-one and latex gloves to deal with Unpleasantness. For foreplay you read the manual to your partner, bookmarking the more complicated passages for ease of on-the-job reference. You only take the photographs as a teaching aid for post-coital debrief, to show your partner precisely what they're doing wrong. When you're finished, you issue them with a compulsory consumer-response form, then run a quick statistical analysis on your in-bed laptop to see how it compares with previous sessions. When asked how it was for you, you deliver a detailed report with bibliography.

Virgo and Mars

As you have discovered (*see page 9*), Mars is planet male; wherever it's belching and scratching in your birthchart determines how you express your Y chromosome. Virgo is the sanctimonious puritan female of the zodiac, so if your Mars is in Virgo as well as your Sun, you have him by his short and curlies. Why waste time having untidy intercourse when you could be having root canal work?

Virgo sex toys

Remote-control vibrator; you are the only sign organized enough not to misplace the remote so that you have to walk around throbbing embarrassingly until the juice runs out.

93

Incompatibility Charts

virgo vs. the rest

Brightsiders say that Virgo (feminine, Earth, mutable, anal-retentive) gets along best with other Earth signs who'll understand (Capricorn and Taurus), and worst with Sagittarius, Pisces, and Gemini (the other mutable chaos magnets). However, this is the Darkside, where everybody is incompatible with everyone else. Here's how.

Virgo and Aries You never know when to stop with your constructive criticism, which is why they are on an assault charge and you are a picture of smug, self-righteous victimhood.

Virgo and Taurus Fellow Earth sign, but you disapprove of their indulgence, and whenever you go out (which is not often), you halve their portions for them and replace their heavy cream with soy.

Virgo and Gemini A mutable sign and ruled by Mercury, just like you, but they always bring on your panic attacks when you go out, because they high-five everyone and never use a hand sanitizer.

Virgo and Cancer When you went back to their place, the dust brought on your asthma, and you had to give them some much-needed guidelines on diet, dress sense, and general cleanliness.

Virgo and Leo A royal no-no. They invite you to a star-studded opening night, with champagne cocktails; you point out the stains on the red carpet and bring your own ginseng tea.

Virgo and Virgo It all falls apart when you discover they have been sneaking into your apartment to reclean the bathroom, while you were at their place doing exactly the same thing.

Virgo and Libra Where would you go? The price of a mint julep at their favorite bar makes you pass out; and they wouldn't be seen dead in your favorite organic wholefood collective.

Virgo and Scorpio Even you can't resist a Scorpio on full beam, but only you could kill the mood stone-dead by pointing out, at the critical moment, that the boil on their butt was about to burst.

Virgo and Sagittarius Another mutable sign, but noisy and gobby where you are neat and candid. The upside is that you get plenty of ops to use your paramedic skills and say, "I told you so."

Virgo and Capricorn A fellow Earth sign, but cardinal, so tries to show you who's boss by being an even cheaper date than you. First to develop hypothermia pays for the rice cakes!

Virgo and Aquarius Something clicks when you meet at an alternative medicine seminar, but when they offer to cure several of your allergies using one of their Jedi mind tricks, you lose your nerve.

Virgo and Pisces The last mutable sign and your opposite; you've never actually had a date, because whatever arrangements you make, they turn up at the wrong place and on the wrong day.

Love rat?

You never rat; it's much worse than that—it's death by analysis. You always want to talk about it. Because you have a database instead of a brain or heart, you remember everything that ever happened in the relationship and refuse to let lovers go until you have gone over every last detail (and not even then). Hag-ridden exes who try to escape are nagged to death (or justifiable homicide) via text, letter, e-mail, and phone.

GETTING BACK AT VIRGO

Virgo is in a constant state of tetch anyway, so you don't have to work too hard. Fun-Tak® magnets to their laptop, water down their Clorox® supply, have Happy Meals™ delivered on the hour. Don't bother with the shrimp in drapes routine, because they clean their drapes weekly.

Your Cheatin' Heart

if only . . .

Successful cheating is all in the detail; and who in the zodiac is better organized for a lifetime of serial adultery and double-dealing than you? You always pack spare underwear and a toothbrush, even if you're only going to the 7-Eleven®. Your electronic diary tells you who you've been with, where and when, and you can reroute all your calls to a secret central number. You remember all the little things; you'd never be caught. Pisces would kill for your skill set; but you can never use it yourself because you can't attract enough lovers.

You combine being dumped with dumping in one smooth, efficient move; you are so hypercritical that lovers think you don't love them any more, and leave before you can explain that you were just trying to get them up to the required standard so that you could propose.

Virgo excuses

You do not do excuses. You are never wrong. When asked why you missed your lover's birthday, it would be a piece of cake for you to prove—with a flipchart and supporting evidence—that they (and their mother) got the date wrong and that you were right.

Virgo pre-nup

Don't mess with Virgo. This is a legally binding document; there is a copy on file with your attorney and three backups locked away in your hard drive. Your lover has no idea what's in it, but you know all the clauses by heart (especially the ones about the bathroom) and will not hesitate to point out how your lover has reneged on them and how disappointed you are, but not surprised.

Venus and Virgo
perfect storm

When Mercury can get away from Gemini, he rules you. Of course, with you he is much more sensible, and in charge of health and safety and communications (bitching). What with your OCD, Venus's vanity, and Mercury's Chronic Busybody Condition, you can't stop yourself coming on like a daytime TV makeover maven, fiddling with details, and fixing stuff that ain't broke. Astrological logistics (*see pages 8–9*) mean that your Venus will be in Virgo, Cancer, Leo, Libra, or Scorpio.

Hot Virgo Role Models

D.H. Lawrence, September 11, 1885
Literature's Mr. Sex, author of *Lady Chatterley's Lover*, a forensic account of sexual intercourse; strutted around Bloomsbury salons telling others how to write, but ran away when criticized.

Greta Garbo, September 18, 1905
Reclusive Swedish screen goddess, who realized early on that other people were simply not good enough, and that it was much more fascinating to be alone.

Venus in Virgo

Venus in Virgo, when you are already Virgo, means that although you may be passionate, you are also a perfectionist who will be awarding points for performance. You slip into your latex catsuit, invite your lover around for an intimate tongue-lashing, and spend a happy evening pointing out that every little thing they do is not good enough.

Venus in Cancer

This is the Tough Love mom placement, so you don't let your lover leave in the morning until you have brushed their collar, retied their shoelaces, inspected their fingernails, and packed them a nourishing tofu 'n' wheatgrass lunchbox. When they don't come back, you call Missing Persons.

Venus in Leo

Here Venus is in the Lady Macbeth position. You're going to thrust greatness on your lover whether they want it or not, so you handcarve a pedestal, insist they take their shoes off before you put them on it, then prowl around with a giant can of spray polish so they daren't get off.

Venus in Libra

Venus is in one of her own signs here, so things are slightly warmer (but not that much). Your boudoir has two en-suite bathrooms: one for ardent incoming lovers and the other for sorrowful outgoing exes. You keep a detailed roster under your pillow.

Venus in Scorpio

Venus in this position is intense, but that's no reason to neglect hygiene. There's nothing wrong with a little depravity, as long as it is properly scrubbed. Your black leather hotpants and stiletto boots sit neatly in their special closet, and your whips are a pleasure to be chastized with.

Libra

September 23–October 23

Hey, gorgeous. Someone as cute and successful as you must be bored with amateurs, the kind of people who won't let you have any fun and just don't know how to wear diamonds. Do you have lots and lots of money, a house in the Hamptons, an apartment on the East Side, and your own Lear jet? Wouldn't you just love to share them with a special, classy, beautifully groomed someone who can make you look really good at important parties and can be relied upon to persuade your shyer business associates to come across? Let me help you; you know you want to. Gender immaterial.

One-night stand

You're all for this in principle (you are the sign of justice after all), and this is the only way all your admirers are going to get a piece of you in one lifetime, but it is rather tiring. You'd much rather stay home on the couch and have them visit you in turn and by appointment.

Two-year stretch

This is a very long time to be celibate (= only one lover) in Libra land and will end in tears—though you get to keep the jewelry. It works much better if you have a 2x2 (two lovers for two years) to keep things beautifully balanced. Remember to dump them both at once.

Long-haul

There's nothing wrong with a marriage of convenience (especially yours). Long-haul can be very lucrative, and can be made quite bearable as long as there are more than two of you on the job. A *ménage à several*, in-house lovers, and serial polygamy are all excellent options.

Libra in Love
love the one you're with

The trouble with falling in love with just one person is that as soon as you do, all other options are closed off; but you like to have your cake, eat it, and keep some in the cake box for later. What to do? You spent some years getting it wrong, then suddenly you realized that all you have to do is fall in love with everybody at the same time! Simple, eh? Everybody fights over you, you never have to make nasty, limiting decisions, there's no heartache (at least, not for you), and you get way more presents and have lots more fun. And you don't have to worry about driving away the one you really love, because the great love of your life is you. You've already got a soulmate to give you cosmic balance—it lives in your mirror.

Stalker?
Playing hard to get, and always being just out of reach, is much more effective; they do all the work, you get all the attention.

Tease?
You are the CEO of Tease International, home of extravagant luxury promises— you never knowingly delivered on any.

Gold digger?
Digger's such a sweaty word; you can separate a client from their cashflow just by smiling across a crowded room.

Scales pickup lines

It's not what you say, it's the way you say it—and who you say it to:
- ♥ Have I got something in my eye?
- ♥ Is that your yacht out in the bay?
- ♥ My zipper's stuck

Dating Libra

multiple choice

Oh, please. You can get a date when you're asleep or dead. You like to batch 'em up: you can't be expected to choose which one you like most, and you have more than enough charm to fuel a rewarding evening with at least a half-dozen lovesick saps, all of whom check their pride in at the door and dance around you like a bunch of second-line hoofers in an Astaire & Rogers movie. They all bring delicious gifts and you can work out who is most cost-effective later.

Once, during an unaccountable dry patch, you tried speed-dating; you worked the room two at a time and naturally they all signed up for you, but it was far too much like hard work.

Your range is much wider than most of the zodiac because it includes the already married or committed. In fact you prefer the sugar daddy/momma option because they stay grateful and generous, and you don't have to put up with all that tedious shouting in the morning about socks and mortgage payments.

Anyone can date Libra as long as they are rich and handsome, poor and stunningly beautiful, or mega rich with a face like chopped liver and the conversational skills of a carpet tile. Where can they find you? Rodeo Drive, red-carpet premières, $2,500-a-plate charity dinners, five-star hotel lobbies, airport VIP lounges, Fifth Avenue.

You let them take you to Spago (you're not paying) and then limo you to exclusive clubs and bars all over town (so you can flirt with your other lovers and leave notes for anyone with potential). You always go to the third date (you know the deal), but ask prettily if you can go to the Four Seasons penthouse because your condo is being feng-shui'd. Of course they always call back.

- incandescent
- burning
- hot
- warm
- cool
- cold
- sub-zero

Libra love token

Something really personal—a lock of your hair, perhaps, doused in your signature scent—but exquisitely giftwrapped. You also like to leave selected trash around (nail clippings, worn underwear, an apple with your perfect teeth marks in it), so that besotted admirers can "steal" it.

Libra online

You're not that interested in online dating because only the poor and desperate use it. You do have your own podcast, though, so all your real-time lovers can get to see you when they want, and it costs them hardly anything. All you have to do is spend time in a luxury hotel room (paid for by a dear friend), lying around in Agent Provocateur looking gorgeous. As you'd be doing that anyway, it's no trouble, and it warms your heart that so many of your lovers log on so often, just to see little ol' you.

What gets Libra hot

You are an Air sign, so it is all sex in the head
with you. So the mere thought of rolling
around in a sea of freshly minted $20 bills, a
dear little Picasso of your own, nights under
the stars on the deck of a luxury yacht, etc.
makes you so weak you have to lie down on
a cashmere and mink rug with a supermodel
for a while. A recurrent fantasy is to pretend
you have never even been kissed before and
let lovers seduce you; it makes a change,
and lets them feel proud and conquering.

Between the sheets

Horizontal, with other people doing the heavy
stuff, and nothing that makes you look ugly.
So no on-top work unless you have just had
your facial peel, but from behind is always
good as you can get on with shaping your
eyebrows. You are not lazy, you just like to
look serene at all times, so you prefer inside
work. One of the reasons lovers flock back
to you is your special version of the Kegel
exercise. And all your lovers praise your
handiwork and your deft little fingers.

Sex with Libra

mirror, mirror

It's all done with mirrors: you flatter and flirt and fondle, but you don't do unbridled passion because that would make you look sweaty and out of control. When you look deep into another's eyes, it's because those dark, lust-dilated pupils make perfectly darling little mirrors and all you can see is the twin reflection of tiny exquisite yous. Divine!

You know everything there is to know about seduction, deferred gratification, and teasing; but by the time you have lit enough candles to constitute a fire hazard, slipped in and out of something more comfortable several times, and reconfigured the satin cushions and velvet throws to your liking, your partner has usually gone to sleep. You don't mind: less mess and more beauty sleep for you, and a fine opportunity to guilt a nice little gift out of them because they left you all on your ownsome.

Libra and Mars

As you have seen (*see page 9*), Mars is planet bigboy—ooh, he is so strong and masterful—and wherever he stands in a manly pose in your birthchart tells you just how buff and executive you are. However, Libra is ruled by Venus, Mars's best girl, so if your Mars is in Libra as well as your Sun, you often find yourself with your pants down and in no position to fight.

Libra sex toys

Lipstick vibrator: small, exquisite, slips discreetly in the purse, and you can retouch as often as you like; the silk love ropes, peacock feathers, velvet padded harnesses, etc. are to please your fans.

Incompatibility Charts
libra vs. the rest

Brightsiders say that Libra (masculine, Air, cardinal, airhead) gets along best with other Air signs who'll understand (Aquarius and Gemini), and worst with Capricorn, Aries, and Cancer (the other cardinal signs trying to wear the zodiacal pants). However, this is the Darkside, where everybody is incompatible with everyone else. Here's how.

Libra and Aries A fellow cardinal and your opposite sign; this thing is bigger than both of you, as you are channeling Venus and Mars (your ruling planets); it's Cathy and Heathcliff all over again.

Libra and Taurus Venus rules both of you, which means you can't fool them quite as easily as you can the rest of us, and you could end up in a gilded cage, the key to which is around their neck.

Libra and Gemini A fellow Air sign, so lots of hard-eyed, flirt-filled encounters promising each other undying love, the world, that you'll call, etc.—but you both know the rules, so there's no harm done.

Libra and Cancer Another cardinal, so you lay on extra charm to form an alliance. However, they won't come out of their shell because they remember how much you didn't deliver last time.

Libra and Leo You are the zodiac's resident groupie, so this gig should be a piece of gâteau, as long as you can train yourself not to fall asleep during the interminable guitar solos.

Libra and Virgo Not a chance. You give them a book of love poetry; they send it back, proofread. They give you a set of self-help manuals; you give it to the help, to use in the cat's litter tray.

Libra and Libra Because you understand each other's game plan only too well, this one will never get past the first date. There's room for only one Libran in your mirror—and it isn't them.

Libra and Scorpio All that beady-eyed intensity is so tiring, not to mention the endless sex; if they weren't so powerful and rich, you just might pass them on to one of your coworkers.

Libra and Sagittarius Your bit of rough: messy and tactless, but always attracts a crowd, so you can slip away with someone a lot more agreeable while they're showing off their fire-eating trick.

Libra and Capricorn Another cardinal to be neutralized and, if possible, scalped. Fortunately this is easy-peasy, because they are the ultimate meal ticket and you are the ultimate trophy spouse.

Libra and Aquarius A fellow Air sign, a chilly-hearted challenge to your charm skills, but fashionwise there's a thin line between cool and dork, and you can't be seen with them when they cross it.

Libra and Pisces A career parasite like you needs a host with an actual backbone, so you soon throw this one back into the pond, usually a couple of drinks into the first date.

Love rat?

You couldn't call it ratting, it's more like plate spinning. You don't like to lose anyone, so keep them on layaway, because you never know when their look may come back into fashion or they may inherit. Ersatz affection comes easy to you, so it's not hard to keep the more lucrative lovers hanging on. You just do a weekly round of flattery and ego massage to keep them all sweet. It's hard work, but pays dividends in the long term.

GETTING BACK AT LIBRA

You are so charmingly slick that most of us don't look for revenge, but berate ourselves for not being good enough— so of course you had to leave. A few self-destruct, hurling themselves from the Golden Gate Bridge screaming your name so that you will feel sorry for what you did. You won't.

Your Cheatiŋ' Heart

shopping around

Unimaginative people might say that you are a constant cheat, but you can't see that at all. Is it cheating to shop for Prada at Bloomingdale's just because Cartier's don't stock it? Or to prefer skiing in Aspen because there's no snow in Miami? You are a professional shopper, and brand loyalty is very important to you (for example, you would never cheat with anyone poor AND plain) but where would the retail sector be if everyone only ever shopped at one place all their life?

You only dump if they fail your annual review. You keep a secret ledger in your head logging favors in/favors out. If they are in deficit, it's Chapter II for them until they have restructured their finances. You always do an exit interview and emphasize their good points so they can do better next time, as you are willing to re-hire once they've upped their game.

Libra excuses

Sweetie-pie, would I lie to you? I was just giving poor Jodie a back rub because it's been a bad day at NYSE and the air conditioner failed, so we had to take our clothes off. Come and join us. Don't you want me to be nice to your best friend?

Libra pre-nup

You are the sign of Justice. Underneath that ditzy exterior you are solid steel, with the law on your side, so your pre-nups are unbreakable. Specifics include your inalienable charge card privileges (valid until you die), a guaranteed minimum spend per date, responsibility (theirs) for your beauty maintenance and wardrobe costs, and your essential non-exclusivity clause.

Venus and Libra

pouting perfection

Venus is in her own luxurious boudoir here: less likely to go out and get it, as she does with Taurus, and more likely to sprawl on a bed of rose petals demanding that it be brought to her—now, with a glass of Krug. With you she comes on strong as the goddess of accessories and pouting, and together you make an Olympic-class Sulking Pair. Astrological logistics (*see page 8*) mean that your Venus will be in Libra, Leo, Virgo, Scorpio, or Sagittarius.

Hot Libra Role Models

Oscar Wilde, October 16, 1864
Wit, aesthete, playwright, and snappy dresser who despised sweaty sports and could resist anything but temptation. Although married with kids, the love of his life was Lord Alfred Douglas.

Lillie Langtry, October 13, 1853
The Jersey Lily, a not-very-good actress, but alpha mistress to many VIPs, including Edward VII of England; always married to someone, but not for long.

Venus in Libra

Venus in Libra, when you are already Libra and Venus rules Libra, is a triple whammy on the love front. It's like being sat on by Barry White, the Walrus of Love. You murmur sweet nothings as you spoon warm honey over the beloveds, so that when you throw yourself at them, nothing can pry you off.

Venus in Leo

Venus in this position never lets you forget she is a goddess with a royal prerogative—the Queen of Hearts. Feel the real power of love. You pounce on your lovers, bat them playfully with your paws (usually velveted), and adore them fiercely until they wilt. If they cross you, you behead them.

Venus in Virgo

In this placing, Venus never messes up her bed or lets lovers mess up her life. You love your beloved to pieces—which you sweep up carefully, categorize, and label in your best calligraphy, then pin out in neat, regimented rows in your specimen case.

Venus in Scorpio

It's intense. Permanently hot and lecherous, you are always up for dirtying the satin sheets in a glossy hotel, preferably with someone illicit and unsuitable, like the bellboy or your sister-in-law, because after sex you love a long, indulgent soak in emotionally muddy waters.

Venus in Sagittarius

This placing drags you and Venus out of bed and into action, so you cover more ground than usual. You swing into the love object's boudoir at midnight on a velvet rope, make passionate (and almost energetic) love, then dash off into the dawn leaving only a hoofprint on their bed and heart.

Scorpio

October 24–November 21

Look into my eyes. Know that I am so powerful
I can bend you to my will without even being
there. Realize that you will not escape and that
resistance is futile. I always get what I want, and
I can wait a very, very long time. We both know
you are fascinated by my effortless power over
the universe and are wetting your underwear over
the thought of hours of wordless, mind-melting
sex in the afternoon in a hot motel room with
beat-up shades, and the whine of the highway
droning in the distance. Don't call me; I get very
angry if my privacy is invaded. I'll find you.

One-night stand

Repeat-action, mindless sex is obviously the solution to your constant craving, but one a night hardly scratches the surface, does it? Unless you're a rock star (and some of you are) with an enterprising roadie, supply can't be guaranteed. Have you thought of turning pro?

Two-year stretch

After the first month you will despise them for being so dependent (but it won't slow down your sex life or make you any less possessive). It takes you the next 23 months to degrade them to the point where they finally leave you. You're incapable of letting go of anything yourself.

Long-haul

This works well because it means you always have someone to manipulate, but make sure they're a robust specimen, or they won't stay the course. You prefer to be the dominant partner, but because you are ultra-cunning you can play subordinate and exploit the tyranny of the weak.

Scorpio in Love
mind games forever

Although constantly in lust, you are rarely in love, and if you are, you make sure we don't catch you at it. You despise the weak; being in love is weak-minded (how could you let another person short-circuit your control systems like that?); therefore when you are in love, you are weak. You must regain control as soon as possible, so that your enemies don't realize you have a vulnerable spot and take advantage—as you would. So you show the world how much in love you're not by locking the beloved away in a remote cabin. They never see or talk to anyone but you, and you only visit under cover of darkness, when you play spiteful mind games so that they won't find out you are in love with them and take advantage.

Stalker?
You've seen birds of prey hovering over a kill? That's you, that is: always just far enough away to avoid a restraining order.

Tease?
It hurts you too, but you sometimes leave lovers unfulfilled, just to show how you can control the uncontrollable.

Gold digger?
Deluded fools line up to shower you with cash, house deeds, etc., but you refuse to give up personal power for a few baubles.

Scorpion pickup lines

You don't need these; you just look at them, leave, and they follow, but just in case:
- ♥ The restroom, two minutes
- ♥ Are you as hot as I am?
- ♥ Don't touch me

Dating Scorpio
supply and demand

If you want a date, you will get one. It doesn't matter if you look like a love god, a cave troll, or a slant-shouldered librarian, you are usually beating them off with a stick: Scorpio magnetism has nothing to do with being ridiculously good-looking. You don't bother with all that flirting and romance and bower-building neediness. Regardless of your actual gender, you become one with the tomcat, stand at certain indefinably arousing angles, your ears go back, your eyes go black, and you focus on the love object, who becomes a rigid rabbit in the glare of your headlights. After that, it's just a question of getting a room.

In theory, speed-dating could have solved your perennial supply problem (sex addiction has the same problem as any other addiction), but a basic misunderstanding of the setup saw you escorted off the premises as soon as you had leaped over the desk onto the first person you sat opposite.

Anyone wanting a little wild side action with no strings should look for you at night, in dark places: jazz cellars, bank vaults, crypts, questionable dockside bars, or your local chapter of Fight Club. If you are a Mr. Big-type Scorpio, you will be cruising the streets in your blacked-out Lexus, and you will find them. If you are on a degradation jag, you'll be under the overpass with your shopping cart.

You don't take your dates anywhere; you like it where you are, so you stay there drinking red wine. Sometimes you wait for the third date, just to show you can. It doesn't really matter where you go, as long as it's not your place, because you refuse to compromise your privacy: so it's out the back of the nightclub, in the back of your limo, a chain motel, or on the roof of the Trump Tower. You never call back.

118

Romance Levels

— incandescent

— burning

— hot

— warm

— cool

— cold

— sub-zero

Scorpio love token

Why should you give them anything? Isn't the scent of your flesh, and the slow trickle in the belly whenever they think of you, enough? Maybe something cheap and tacky made precious by the fact that you never usually give gifts? That'll keep them in your power.

Scorpio online

Going online gives you complete control (yes, yes!); you can be whatever gender you like, fantasize darkly until even you feel a bit weird, pick up all sorts of information that unwary fools post, and use it against them, yet keep your own info secret and hidden behind a byzantine system of passwords and firewalls. Your profile gets 2K hits a week. Online dating is a neat solution if you are out of action: in rehab, holed up on a stakeout, in a Zen monastery having one of your self-denial weeks, or on Death Row.

119

What gets Scorpio hot

Well, what doesn't? You are on permanent heat, lust motes dancing before your eyes, and have to disappear regularly to get some satisfaction before you start rubbing up against fire plugs. You like illicit action with people you shouldn't be with, in places you shouldn't be, at times when you should be somewhere else. You know all about the link between sex and death, and can't help yourself coming on to the grieving widow/er at funerals; they rarely turn you down.

Between the sheets

You've done absolutely everything so it's hard to say, but you can narrow it down to three categories. When you are overcome, there's the fast-action up-against-the wall or in-a-crowded-subway-car option. When you just can't get enough degradation, you go for handcuffed-to-the-dumpster-and-doused-in-bootleg-jack look. Mostly, because you love to show how in control you are, it's the tantric one where you are on one leg and they are upside down, and you keep it up for hours.

Sex with Scorpio
power trip

You can't help it (not that you try very hard): Scorpio rules the genitals, so you are just following your hormones. How convenient for you, because sex is power (what you really, really want), and your tuning fork vibrates exactly with the bat's squeak of desire that drives the world.

Everybody knows that sex with Scorpio is intense, passionate, throbbing, etc., but you are just the same when you are on your own. It's the sex you love, not the one you're with. While you are often almost blind with lust, you are always in charge, and sex is on your terms only. You might want serial one-night stands; you might want intense, constant, obsessional sex with one erotic muse. You might even want to show how in control of control you are, by giving up sex altogether for a life of hot-eyed celibacy, sweetened by twice-daily scourging sessions alone with your ground-glass-encrusted flail.

Scorpio and Mars

As you have discovered (*see page 9*), Mars is planet power, and wherever it plugs in to your birthchart reveals just how menacing and determined you are. You used to be ruled by Mars, and he still remembers, even if you think he's just a bit of loud muscle, little brain, and even less class; so if your Mars is in Scorpio as well as your Sun, you are the star recidivist at the Sex Addiction Clinic.

Scorpio sex toys

It's not a game, you know; well, maybe some tight leather and a knife to cut you out of it. Your shameful, uncool, secret passion is baked goods; think *American Pie*.

Incompatibility Charts
scorpio vs. the rest

Brightsiders say that Scorpio (feminine, Water, fixed, obsessive) gets along best with other Water signs who'll understand (Pisces and Cancer), and worst with Aquarius, Leo, and Taurus (the other fixed signs who insist we all do it their way). However, this is the Darkside, where everybody is incompatible with everyone else. Here's how.

Scorpio and Aries They are ruled by Mars, and you used to be; so on any date you both stumble about in a competitive red mist trying to outlust each other. Where's your legendary self-control?

Scorpio and Taurus Another fixed sign and your unlikely opposite. Neither of you will give in, which is why you brood in a bistro in Paris, France, while they wait for you in a diner in Paris, Texas.

Scorpio and Gemini You are intense and possessive and will kill anyone who looks at your date; they are the zodiac's flirt. Keep away, or it will be a bloodbath followed by Death Row for you.

Scorpio and Cancer A fellow Water sign, with worse moods and a longer memory for past hurts, so it can be a very long night staring into your Pinot Noir waiting for one of you to snap out of it.

Scorpio and Leo A fellow fixed sign, but Fire; nicely steamy for a while, it soon fades because you won't tell then how wonderful they are, or sign a release form so that they can show the clip on MTV.

Scorpio and Virgo After 24 hours of what you thought was mutually delicious degradation and dominance, you wake up to find them sniffily steam-pressing the whips and polishing the jackboots.

Scorpio and Libra They love a challenge, and your all-black wardrobe is such a good look, but they drop you when you get all intense and controlling on them and refuse to go shopping.

Scorpio and Scorpio It's like magnets: either you lock onto each other inseparably and die of sex, or you repel each other totally and die fighting. Either way, it always clears the room.

Scorpio and Sagittarius Because you can't control them, you turn up your nose. More fool you, for they have great stamina and can service your insatiable sex addiction without breaking a sweat.

Scorpio and Capricorn You, above all signs, can lure out their inner goat for some serious naughtiness, but in the morning their outer accountant denies it all and slaps on a gagging order.

Scorpio and Aquarius The last fixed sign. Not only can you not bend them to your will, but they are quite happy to argue logically about it all night long, when all you want is some silent sex.

Scorpio and Pisces The final Water sign, and needily eager to collude with you in anything sordid—except your addiction to restraint and self-denial. Denial means something else to Pisces.

Love rat?

You are well aware of the difference between love and sex—which is why you make such a hot sex worker and take the highest number of booty calls in the zodiac—but you don't care if others aren't. They are weak, so of course you take advantage, otherwise *you* would look weak. The world is littered with Scorpio discards (usually Pisceans) who believed that a 12-hour lustfest meant it was time to start choosing drapes.

GETTING BACK AT SCORPIO

Don't do this (unless you are another Scorpio prepared to take it to the death). Suck it up; roll with it; you will never win. If you do nothing, at least you will slightly unnerve them, because they will be expecting you to try something laughably inept and will look forward to destroying you.

Your Cheatin' Heart

jealous guy

Only weak people cheat. It is tawdry and commonplace. Being tempted with the promise of exquisite, illicit ecstasy, and resisting—now that's what I call control. If that's not enough manipulation for you, try scattering a few careless clues about to make them think you are cheating when you're not, and watch all that pain and agony being suffered because of you; you could end it all in a minute with an explanatory word, but where would be the fun in that?

However, if you suspect they may be cheating on you, you morph into the CSI team on triple time, sniffing their clothes, reading their diaries, going over their vehicle with that special flashlight that shows up sexual-activity traces, rerouting their cellphone via yours, planting homing devices in the heels of all their shoes, etc. Then you kill them. No one dumps you.

Scorpio excuses

If anyone's reckless enough to ask you to explain yourself, you glare at them until they hyperventilate. You can panic other people into making lame, unconvincing excuses for things they haven't even done, without leaving a mark on them.

Scorpio pre-nup

Not strictly necessary, for who would disobey your will, but you like to reinforce all potential weak spots, so this will be in triplicate and signed in blood (theirs). There are few clauses, but they are all ironclad: they are to do exactly what you order at all times; they must be available for sex whenever you feel like it; they must not step outside the circle of power you have drawn around them.

Venus and Scorpio

dynamite

Modern astros say that your ruler is cold, distant, psychopathic Pluto, but according to old-schoolers, you were once ruled by Mars. So underneath all that power-crazed manipulating, you are atavistic raw sex. And we know how Venus feels about Mars; imagine what happens when they are strapped together in the hot, airless confines of your sign. Astrological logistics (*see pages 8–9*) mean that your Venus will be in Scorpio, Virgo, Libra, Sagittarius, or Capricorn.

Hot Scorpio Role Models

Pablo Picasso, October 25, 1881
Passionate, prolific, seminal, shaping spirit of 20th-century art, famous for his ability to analyze and synthesize, as well as for his magnetic stare and his atrocious, compulsive womanizing.

Vivien Leigh, November 5, 1913
Adequately talented but ferociously focused English actress who stole the juicy role of Scarlett O'Hara from under the noses of the Hollywood A-list.

126

Venus in Scorpio

Venus in Scorpio, when you are already Scorpio, means you should only be allowed out on cold nights and should always carry your own bucket of water to throw over yourself. You can't live without intensive, relentless, steaming, get-a-room sex on the hour, anyplace, anywhere, with anyone. It would be a crime of passion to dilute your drive with flirting or foreplay, and your lust slaves know better than to ask.

Venus in Virgo

This is the Nurse Whiplash placing, which means that you get to scrub up before lots of strenuous, bracing, vigorous sex (with regular shower breaks) on rubber sheets. You can use your stethoscope to chastise lovers who muss up your crisp white uniform.

Venus in Libra

Venus is in one of her own signs here, softening your trademark power glare with a slick of smoky eye shadow, but you still demand intense, languid, romantic sex with slidey satin sheets and pretty acolytes strewing rose petals and mint leaves. A partner isn't necessary.

Venus in Sagittarius

This placing turns Venus into a frisky dark horse, a tiring combination of intensity and physical energy. Every sexual encounter turns into a race, and you are very keen on competitive lustathons you can place bets on: the fastest gallop through the *Kama Sutra*, the four-minute orgasm, etc.

Venus in Capricorn

Strictly business. Unbutton that three-piece suit, take off your specs, and get down to some intense, serious sex on the solid mahogany boardroom table of an old, established merchant bank with an old, established merchant banker.

Sagittarius

November 22–December 21

Bored with life? Looking for an "unstable" mate? (See what I did there? That's my Most Excellent GSOH in action! Now you know what you're in for, I bet you can't wait—what odds can you give me?) Restless, unreliable riskophiliac and founder member of GA WLTM a gang of Russian-roulette players, for serial, very short, but adrenaline-soaked relationships, preferably while downhill racing. Indiscretion guaranteed. Update your insurance, because I don't have any, and bring your own hip flask—I lost mine when I was subway surfing.

One-night stand

What's not to like? It delivers an invigorating workout to keep your body ripped, avoids messy commitment issues, doesn't take up too much good gambling/ drinking time—and you never get bored. Of course, you always take precautions: you never give your real name.

Two-year stretch

You are very sociable, and working as a team, especially pulling a smart wagon, can be fun for a while; then you come to a crossroads, you bolt one way, they go the other, and the wagon hits the rocks. You are found later peacefully drinking at a bar, as if nothing had happened.

Long-haul

This is only going to work if you've been put out to grass and are too old or spavined to jump the fence, or you are an international explorer/ freedom fighter who is never at home; the media will remind you who your partner is at regular intervals, and you can write loving letters.

Sagittarius in Love

constantly inconstant

Everyone knows when you're in love, usually because we are Maced by the nimbus of pheromones that sticks around after you've gone, like cheap aftershave. Then there's the ardent clattering and snorting. Where we go wrong is thinking that the love object is a constant. On Monday, you pace the room swishing your tail, knock over a few small pieces of furniture, and tell us how much you love Beavis (say), what a wonderful and perfect human being they are, and how you are not worthy. On Wednesday, we ask how it's going with Beavis and you stare at us in genuine bafflement and say, "Who?" because now you are besotted with Butt-head, who is a wonderful and perfect human being, etc.

Stalker?

How? Stalking requires patience, stealth, an attention span, and long-term planning, none of which you possess.

Tease?

You prance about irritatingly, withholding favors only because it makes it more fun when you let go. It's fun—lighten up.

Gold digger?

No, but when you've splashed all your own cash and nuked your plastic, you freeload without guilt or mercy.

Archer pickup lines

Oh dear, better to shut up and let your animal magnetism do the work:
- If I said you had a beautiful body, would you hold it against me?
- Do you think I'm sexy?
- Nice buns!

131

Dating Sagittarius
odds-on favorite?

Self-belief is all; you are convinced you have the pulling power of a plowhorse on prednisone. Surely just one flash of your big, handsome teeth makes you everyone's favorite for the big race? If the punters don't bite, you don't return to your stable to sulk with your ego in pieces; you just take a canter around the block and approach the fence from a different angle, with more force. You like to lay bets with your buddies on whether or not you will score, and when. You have finally learned not to tell datees about this, but don't understand why, because you always get great odds, which means you can take them somewhere way classier than your usual Mickey D's.

They misled you about speed-dating; what's with the sitting down? Where's the speed? Two whole minutes with each candidate? And you're all corralled in one place for how long? I don't think so.

You will date absolutely anyone, but people who have taken out extra medical insurance who like a vigorous workout, combined with "hilarious" practical jokes, elaborate windups, terrible puns, and maybe some slight scorching, will be onto a sure thing. You are easy to find: up an Alp, skydiving, rigging the slots in Vegas, betting the farm at Churchill Downs, free climbing the Hancock Tower, or in the ER.

You like to show them a good time, so you run a red to engineer a police chase (you win), and go to Little Tokyo to eat that Japanese fish that kills you if not prepared properly. Your hooves may get too itchy to hang around for the Third Date, but if you do, you go to their place, because you haven't got one and not everybody wants to sleep out under the stars in a buddy's yurt. You call when you're next in town; they're married to someone else, but that won't stop you.

Sagittarius love token

Anything inappropriate and embarrassing will do for you. A blood-soaked Band-Aid® between the sheets. A rash. A fractured rib. The starey, scary, megasized cuddly toy you won at the traveling show shooting gallery. His 'n' Hers Heelys®, with monograms. Your used betting slips.

incandescent

burning

hot

warm

cool

cold

sub-zero

Sagittarius online

It's boring filling out that personal info profile, and you can never remember what you said last time (or your passwords). Much more fun just to surf the sites, usually on somebody else's laptop (you just borrowed it, OK?; they were asleep). Basically you are blagging stopovers in as many places as you can and don't mind how you pay for it. You get lots of hits on your sex-on-a-snowboard YouTube clip, but because you posted it using a buddy's account, never get to follow them up.

What gets Sagittarius hot

You love the smell of Gore-Tex® and Neoprene in the morning, so anybody who wheelslides to your feet dressed in a wetsuit with a roll of gripper tape between their teeth is talking your language—as is anyone with VIP access to Wrigley Field for a midnight midpitch session. On wet nights when you have to stay in, one of your favorite fantasies is rolling around blindfold in a sea of poker chips along with a celebrity shark-hunter whose harpoon safety catch is unreliable.

Between the sheets

As long as you are in motion that's fine by you: so lashed together in a freefall tandem parachute drop; down-hill racing in the spoons position; on the bench seat of your vintage Lincoln Continental (you know, the one with the suicide doors); face to face on your Harley hog. If you are lucky enough to be still in traction from the last time you tried this, take advantage of the fact that you are tied up and that your partner can inflict pain or pleasure just by yanking on your pulley.

Sex with Sagittarius

mustang silly

Hey man, let's burn rubber! What else are glow-in-the-dark comedy condoms for? Sex with you is not for the unbuff; not everybody can swing from the trapeze by their ankles in that nonchalant way you have, and not everybody wants to be somebody else's bench-press buddy. Nor is it for those who need soft lights, sweet music, and satin bedwear to get it on: you're still using your Teenage Mutant Ninja Turtle sheets, and your idea of foreplay is a pillow fight.

You like to big yourself up about leaving 'em breathless, but don't realize they're meant to be weak with spent passion, not exhausted, with lactic-acid buildup in muscles they didn't know they had. But you're not a complete heartless jackhammer; you always give your partner a friendly slap on the haunches while you're doing your post-coital cooldown stretches.

Sagittarius and Mars

As you have seen (*see page 9*), Mars is planet raunch, and wherever it is rutting in your birthchart shows just how thrusting and invincible you are. Your ruler is Jupiter, Mars's old man, so if your Mars is in Sagittarius as well as your Sun, it's like you're on a permanent father-and-son male bonding weekend with antler-locking and don't-tell-mom visits to the cathouse.

Sagittarius sex toys

You can get really playful with just a carrot, but what about hilarious his 'n' hers strap-ons, a hilarious chocolate schlong, or a hilarious whip-and-bridle set for My Little Pony fun?

Incompatibility Charts

sagittarius vs. the rest

Brightsiders say that Sagittarius (masculine, Fire, mutable, ADHD) gets along best with other Fire signs who'll understand (Aries and Leo), and worst with Pisces, Gemini, and Virgo (the other mutable signs who just can't stand still). However, this is the Darkside, where everybody is incompatible with everyone else. Here's how.

Sagittarius and Aries A fellow Fire sign, so the bedroom will be burned to a cinder; the kind of affair that works best under enemy fire in a war zone, and causes mayhem back home in Iowa.

Sagittarius and Taurus Are you even in the same time zone? By the time they have got settled and finally chosen their starter, you've finished all the after-dinner mints and left town.

Sagittarius and Gemini Another mutable sign and your opposite; even on the Darkside, you two are twin souls. They're so smart and you're so up for it, you don't care if you drive over a cliff.

Sagittarius and Cancer You love a milf (or a dilf), but it all gets too close to home when they ground you after bailing you out, again, then take your car keys and stop your allowance.

Sagittarius and Leo Another Fire sign, but fixed, so although they won't go backpacking around Asia with you in case there are no hairdryers, throw a hissy fit when you go with someone else.

Sagittarius and Virgo A fellow Team Mutable player, so you listen to their complicated game plan for the evening for at least 10 seconds before doing what you were going to do anyway.

Sagittarius and Libra They make you feel sweaty and want to show off, so you take them to the racetrack and teach them how to bet; their choices romp home and so do they—with your money.

Sagittarius and Scorpio This would be like Joey Tribbiani (you) dating Hillary Clinton (them). You have no idea of their hidden depths and they can't believe your obvious shallows. Cut your losses.

Sagittarius and Sagittarius Dumb and Dumber. On the first date you dare each other to jack a Hummer®, and the next thing you know, you wake up in Vegas PD. Could it get any more fun?

Sagittarius and Capricorn This feels too much like dating the boss, so of course you blow it spectacularly, bringing water bombs and firecrackers to liven up the first date (*La Traviata* at the Met).

Sagittarius and Aquarius They like to be perverse, so may parade you around their favorite boho salons as a sort of performing party animal; you don't care as long as there's a free lunch.

Sagittarius and Pisces A mutable sign, but wet where you're fiery. Could last to a second date, because you can drink as much as they can, and your ears aren't tuned to their whine-bandwidth.

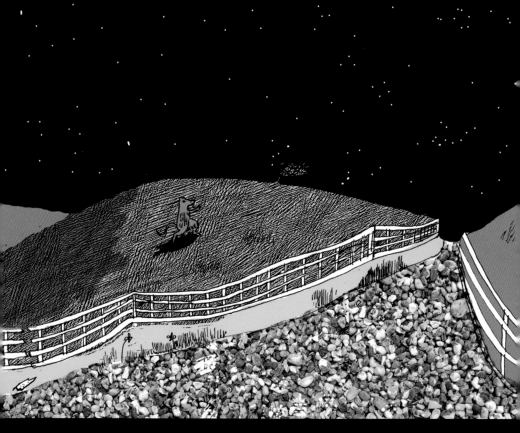

Love rat?

It's not ratting (semantics again), because
you are deluding no one. If the rest of the
zodiac can't read body language that simply
screams "bolter," that's their problem. You will
always slip away in the night, no matter how
many darling little picket fences your partners
try to put up around you, because you don't
do routine and boredom. Any hint of jealousy,
possessiveness, or controlling behavior (e.g.
Shall we do lunch?) and you're off.

GETTING BACK AT SAGITTARIUS

Well, you'd have to find them first. And
why waste time and energy doing stuff
they won't even notice? Avoid obvious
stunts, like sabotaging their bungee
lines or slashing their brake cables, for
the resulting adrenaline surge would
be a reward, not a punishment. Think
limitation: give them up to the IRS.

Your Cheatin' Heart
define your terms

It's a fair cop, you neigh winsomely when caught in a jacuzzi with 24 pole dancers and the local football team. You're a centaur: your head and your heart may say stay, but your hooves and the rest of your equipment are go. What can you do? You play away because you can't resist the adventure; even when supplied with top-grade organic hand-rolled oats at home, you'll still stick your nose into exotic foreign nosebags just for a new taste experience. And, semantically speaking, you're not really cheating; as you point out (usually on your way out, otherwise people throw stuff at you), every statement of love you make is true at the time you make it, but the expression of a sentiment in a statement does not imply that the sentiment *per se* continues for longer than the duration of the statement. You don't notice if anyone cheats on you.

Sagittarius excuses

You're always caught out because you never bother to hide what you're doing. Then it's a disarming shrug, humbling motions, remorseful face, shy cheeky smile, "Aw baby, you know what I'm like; I can't help myself," followed by forgiveness. It's called double bluffing.

Sagittarius pre-nup

Strictly no paperwork, that's your golden rule. It only leads to trouble and lawyers. Your unilateral verbal agreement with everyone is no commitment, no rules, no expectations. On consideration, even that sounds a bit restrictive, so you've added a clause pointing out that nothing you say—not even this clause—can ever be construed as binding in any way at all, legally or otherwise.

Venus and Sagittarius

spoilt rotten

Your ruler is Jupiter, the jolly gas giant. It's named for the father of the gods, and one of the goddesses he is father of is Venus. So when she is with you, Venus is Daddy's Little Princess, the Veruca Salt of the cosmos. You indulge her every whim and smile when she breaks your playdate's heart accidentally on purpose. She can get you to do anything she wants—and you let her. Astrological logistics (*see pages 8–9*) mean that your Venus will be in Sagittarius, Libra, Scorpio, Capricorn, or Aquarius.

Hot Sagittarius Role Models

Jimi Hendrix, November 27, 1942
Restless, iconic guitar god, burned up the stage at Monterey Pop and gave the world *Foxy Lady* and *Electric Ladyland*. Died young and pretty and probably by accident, far away from home.

Mary, Queen of Scots, Dec 8, 1542
Impulsive, indiscreet, adored nearly-Queen, with far too many lovers and husbands; used to escape to nighttime Edinburgh disguised as a stable boy.

Venus in Sagittarius

Venus in Sagittarius, when you are already Sagittarius, doubles your addiction to love on the move and makes you Queen of the Bolters. Mug Cupid, steal a bunch of arrows, and fire them at random. Swoop down on the wounded like a thoroughbred steed, feed them grapes and palm wine, and shag them senseless. As the sun rises over the purple desert sand, gallop off alone.

Venus in Libra

Venus is in her own sign here; how spoiled can one girl get? Toss your silky mane until you have gathered together an admiring herd, then run away with the one who offers the most sugar cubes and the biggest stable (but get the names of the also-rans).

Venus in Scorpio

This is the equestrian porn placing. Saddle up, add a tight bridle, and whip your lover and yourself to ecstasy with your riding crop. Don't forget to negotiate good odds beforehand on who comes first, and how many times.

Venus in Capricorn

In this placing Venus puts the Princess on the back burner and shows Daddy that those Harvard college fees were worth it. Mating is a serious business, so before you do anything rash, you send off for the relevant stud books to compare form. Then you do something rash, but with a high yield.

Venus in Aquarius

Venus in this placing makes you a little less noisy, obvious, and brash, but just as energetic. So you pose enigmatically against the dusk skyline until you intrigue a soulful lover. Then you gallop off with them into the night, get out your enormous telescope, and show them the glories of the horsehead nebula.

Capricorn

December 22–January 19

Respectable, solvent, ambitious businessperson
WLTM someone exactly the same, only more so,
for long-term merger that will enhance our joint
revenue streams and yield beneficial tax breaks.
If you like long walks in the rain, trolling thrift shops,
reading back copies of *The Tightwad Gazette* on
the public library microfiche, and comparing interest
rates for fun and profit, then send in your résumé,
bank statements for the last three months (or your
last set of certified books), together with a handling
fee of $10, and I will get back to you as soon as
I get clearance from TransUnion.

One-night stand

While this saves greatly on heating bills, you often lose concentration because you feel bad about wasting so much time on fun when you could be at home, switching your savings to much higher-yielding accounts. However, your inner goat likes this one a lot, especially on Sundays.

Two-year stretch

This strategy is excellent for bench-testing potential applicants for long-haul. Two years gives you plenty of time to run a thorough background check and establish whether they are worth further investment. Learn not to tell them this, or it will get very nasty.

Long-haul

Now you're talking—it's not about fun or settling down with the love of your life; it's about moving up. Marrying (get it in writing) into class, money, and connections secures a stable basecamp that will make the scramble up the social ladder so much easier on the hooves.

Capricorn in Love
strictly business

The rest of the zodiac have to tell you when you're in love, because you think it's just heartburn or IBS. Then you'll deny it, because love is not the kind of thing you fall in. If you did, you might do something stupid and spontaneous in public, and people would point and jeer, and maybe it would affect your credit rating. You have to be cautious, because you hate wasting your precious time with the wrong person, or, even worse, falling for Somebody Unsuitable. On the other hand, deep inside you are a goat, and goats are capricious and lust-crazed, so you could surprise everybody by running off with a junkie rock star—but it would have to be a junkie rock star with money, talent, and status.

Stalker?
No, but you might hire a private investigator to check out whether they're as all that as they say they are.

Tease?
Your inner goat won't let you; it enjoys sex far too much to miss any chance of serious action just to score points.

Gold digger?
No, just pragmatic; if it's a choice between someone loaded and someone merely solvent, loaded wins every time.

Goat pickup lines

You're looking to trade up, so use these to see if you're on the right track:

💜 Talking about pensions, is yours index-linked or unit trust?
💜 Who's your daddy?
💜 Uh, huh, huh!

Dating Capricorn
social climbing

Dates say that they have a subliminal sensation of being interviewed; this is because they are: you are a social mountaineer, and dating the right person is essential to the climb strategy. If they show talent, stamina, and pedigree, they may get to third date; if not, you e-mail them telling them the post has been filled. You don't want time-wasters, so you arrange meetings via a reputable agency, trusted family members, or a professional matchmaker. (Your goat, when let out, will date any sleazeball with a bottle and a backstage pass.)

Speed-dating cuts waffle and waste, and allows you to maximize impact by pitching to 30 clients at once, but you are not impressed with the quality control. Apparently anybody can join in if they've got the entrance fee.

You're never short of a partner because you are surprisingly desirable, especially to Libra, who knows a meal ticket when they see one. Fans can find you at company freebies, ambassadorial receptions, the lobby of the Federal Reserve, or Black Sabbath gigs (you have a thing for Heavy Metal). Your goat can be found in mosh pits, or at warehouse raves and Satanic rituals.

Since you never do front-loaded investment, you take them for an early lunch to the hot-dog vendor on your work plaza, where you quiz them about their academic qualifications, fiscal status, and pension plans, then whisk them off for a very long (free) walk in the park. As dusk falls, you shake hands and hurry home to check their family tree and credit rating. By the third date you have sorted the wheat from the chaff, and let the goat have its way with the chaff; you and the wheat go to their place (to check that it's a choice digs). You always call.

Romance Levels

- incandescent
- burning
- hot
- warm
- cool
- cold
- sub-zero

Capricorn love token

No need to waste money here; you don't believe in spoiling people, and have your own take on treating them mean to keep 'em keen. How about an almost past-the-use-by-date box of candy from the discount store? Or a novelty keyring snapped up at your neighbor's yard sale?

Capricorn online

Online dating is cost-effective; it avoids all the unaccountable randomness of the real world, and you don't have to spend a dime on dates until you have narrowed it down to a handful of gilt-edged picks that will repay investment. You can find out all their details for free without pissing them off (it does, don't ask you why), and can run your actuarial software alongside to check their shelf life. Plus you can also access hardcore porn; you and the goat watch it together.

147

What gets Capricorn hot

You avoid getting hot—it is undignified and you haven't factored cleaning bills into your weekly microbudget—but can't help yourself at the thought of status sex with someone socially superior and more experienced than you, who will teach you everything they know and maybe let you wear the gimp mask. Your goat fantasizes about group sex around the pentangle in your basement with the Mayor, the Dean, the Police Chief, the Judge, the Senator, and a couple of Reverends.

Between the sheets

This is never anything fancy as you fly strictly no-frills. You like to be on top of everything at work, and you of all people are not about to change the habits of a lifetime, so on top is your preferred MO, with permitted variations. Sometimes you have to use your whip to prevent deviationist behavior from over-imaginative partners. It gives you no pleasure. Your nimble Goat likes to be upwardly mobile, so you sometimes appear on a ladder at your lover's window.

Sex with Capricorn

hidden depths

Traditional is fine by you, so once a week it's pj pants off and lights out as you buckle down to your contractual obligations. It's all over very quickly because you know exactly what is going to happen and when, and so does your partner. Look, you know how to turn them on—it was all worked out right at the beginning—so why would you want to invest time that you could be using more profitably in learning new ways?

That's the cover story you want us all to swallow; but everybody knows that the filthiest things go on in the 'burbs, not the inner city, and underneath that ultra-respectable, buttoned-down façade lurks your inner goat—a randy, lascivious, long-eyed lecher, notorious for its stamina, unquenchable lust, and voracious appetite. That's why partners stay with you, much to everyone's amazement—it's always the quiet ones.

Capricorn and Mars

As you know (*see page 9*), Mars is the planet of getting-things-done, and wherever it is in your birthchart highlights just how determined and goal-oriented you are. You are the sign of discipline and hard grind, which slows Mars down a bit, so if Mars is in Capricorn as well as your Sun, lovers often feel they are having their six-monthly review rather than hot sex.

Capricorn sex toys

Toys are an unnecessary expense, and may not be tax-deductible, but your goat likes blindfolds, and dripping hot wax from black candles onto bare skin to make pagan symbols.

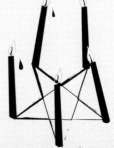

Incompatibility Charts

capricorn vs. the rest

Brightsiders say that Capricorn (feminine, Earth, cardinal, ruthless) gets along best with other Earth signs who'll understand (Taurus and Virgo), and worst with Aries, Cancer, and Libra (the other cardinal signs who want to be CEO of Zodiac, Inc.). However, this is the Darkside, where everybody is incompatible with everyone else. Here's how.

Capricorn and Aries A rival cardinal, but easy to overrule, because they let you handle the money and the paperwork while they do important stuff, like the barbecue and fighting off wolves.

Capricorn and Taurus An Earth associate, with obstinacy levels like yours; you could starve to death on the first date because they insist on à la carte and you insist on PB&J sandwiches.

Capricorn and Gemini They know all about the goat and will tease it out with flattery and tequilas, take photographs, and blackmail you. You know they will, but you can't help yourself.

Capricorn and Cancer Another cardinal and your opposite sign. They try to control the relationship by being late for every date, because they know it makes you mad. They succeed.

Capricorn and Leo Excuse me, what happened to your self-respect? Just because they say their daddy is one of the Forbes 400, it doesn't mean they are. It's called acting. Stop groveling.

Capricorn and Virgo An Earth colleague, but not in a good way, because nothing either of you do will ever be good enough for the other one, so it's more cost-effective not even to start.

Capricorn and Libra The last cardinal sign, but smart enough to convince you that you are running the show, so that they can do whatever they want with you (and your offshore funds).

Capricorn and Scorpio Best to keep this strictly business, with a schedule and a budget, otherwise you'll both try to control each other's soul—and one of you will lose. It won't be them.

Capricorn and Sagittarius Your inner goat loves them, but your outer auditor's blood runs even colder than usual after you have made a credit check and found out they are uninsurable.

Capricorn and Capricorn Where can this go? First you try to outclass each other, then you try to out-cheapskate each other: stalemate. And if both goats get out, there'll be the Devil to pay.

Capricorn and Aquarius You are Captain Sensible, they are a rebel without a cause. They stick around, because you make them look even more of an eccentric loner than they actually are.

Capricorn and Pisces They flatter you into taking the parent role so that they can blame you when it all goes wrong—which it will when you catch them swigging your rare single malt.

Love rat?

It's hard to tell, because few people ever even know they are the object of your affection (and therefore prospective dumpees), and you like to keep it that way. You are a serious person, and any ratting you do is strictly business; deep inside your pre-nup is a clause (unreadable through rose-colored eyewear) that allows you to trade up to someone higher on the social scale, with more money and property, if conditions apply.

GETTING BACK AT CAPRICORN

You won't get to them financially (too ironclad), so play on their obsession with status and hit them where it hurts: at work. Tell everyone their daddy is a longshoreman; e-mail their CEO with a shot of them schmoozing the company rivals (what else is Photoshop® for?); pimp their discreet black VW.

Your Cheatin' Heart
what heart?

Finding your tiny little heart is hard enough, let alone ferreting out whether or not it is cheating. It's very unlikely. You like security and order, and believe that marriage is a fine institution, a sensible way to tie up money and property, and you're not about to jeopardize important stuff like that on something as trivial and self-indulgent as a fling with someone just because they're cute. You deal with the goat either by joining a secret hierarchical society of other consenting goats, which in no way impinges on your relationship (see pre-nup), or by strictly commercial transactions with Scorpio. You very rarely dump, because you have a binding agreement and don't want to incur unnecessary legal fees. If betrayed yourself, your revenge is terrible and reaches down the generations, because it usually involves financial ruin.

Capricorn pre-nup

You're on home ground here, for planning ahead and covering every base are what rocks your boat. Apart from the standard triple-strength titanium cladding, clauses include one that allows you to take your roll-up electronic calculator to bed, and a secret, fiendishly clever time-bomb clause, which means they end up with nothing and you get everything— whichever way they move.

Capricorn excuses

Whatever the complaint, you simply bike over the relevant pages of the pre-nup, highlighted to show that you are entirely blameless, and include a fat invoice to cover your admin costs. The goat does what it likes and doesn't give a damn.

153

Venus and Capricorn

curb your enthusiasm

Venus has a bit of a hard time with you, because you are ruled by Saturn, the no-frills spoilsport, who cuts her clothes allowance and doesn't do indulgence. Basically, he is a curmudgeonly old grandad; however, like many curmudgeonly old grandads, he can be a lechy old goat at times, and that's when you and Venus get jiggy in the most surprising ways. Astrological logistics (*see pages 8–9*) mean that your Venus will be in Capricorn, Scorpio, Sagittarius, Aquarius, or Pisces.

Hot Capricorn Role Models

Elvis Presley, January 8, 1935
The King. Pelvis-swiveling rock god, still hot despite being dead for 30 years. So, one in the eye for everybody who thinks Ebenezer Scrooge and Chairman Mao are all you got.

Marlene Dietrich, December 27, 1901
Cross-dressing, bisexual cabaret artiste and Hollywood icon; the highest-paid actress of her time, and companion and mistress to topline politicos. Übergoat.

Venus in Capricorn

Venus in Capricorn, when you are already Capricorn, makes you either the dullest thing between the sheets or the zodiac's least-expected lust-fiend. Unsuspicious targets, who anticipate nothing more than a stupefying evening sipping warm water and comparing the performance of mutual offshore funds against long-term unit trusts, are in for a big surprise when you flash your cloven hooves at them.

Venus in Scorpio

Venus in this position combines insatiable lust, obsessive control, and a fixation with status and hierarchy. So you are founder and president of your local Satanic Society and get first choice of all the virgins who willingly offer themselves to the Horned One.

Venus in Sagittarius

In this placing Venus gets a bit more skittish, while keeping her eye firmly on the bottom line. Between conferences at the Shanghai Bank, pull the love object into the glass-walled elevator, press the Up button and feel the earth move away.

Venus in Aquarius

This is the Mr. Cool position. Get your people to call their people to find a time slot that fits your separate agendas. Schedule a two-minute lust-window. Fulfill obligations while checking the Dow Jones averages via your Bluetooth®.

Venus in Pisces

This combines the wheedle power of an eight-year-old girl with the mind of a tax lawyer. Play hard to get by dodging elusively behind the more accessible rocks, then let yourself be caught and tied, bleating prettily until a pre-nup is agreed. Behave so badly with their best friends that they are forced to leave you; then sue for breach of contract.

Aquarius

January 20–February 18

Researcher into the human condition, with a special
interest in mating rituals and bonding customs,
WLTM interesting subjects and material to expand
existing database. I'm looking for contributions
from all ages, genders, classes, or species, and
group applications are especially welcome. Don't
worry if you live in another time zone—you can
give me everything I need via my Web site; I won't
be giving you anything. Any feelings of warmth
or affection that you may experience during the
course of the program will not be reciprocated,
and you are responsible for your own therapy fees.

One-night stand

This is a really efficient way to amass data. Because you are friendly, outgoing, and an equal-ops seducer, you can gather a respectable sample (covering all genders and a wide age range) in a very short time. Is it your fault they believed you were interested in them for themselves?

Two-year stretch

Although you welcome a chance to go deep cover and collect significant information on human mating rituals, you could do without all the needy fuss, the clinging to your knees, and the begging when you terminate the experiment after two years, exactly on schedule.

Long-haul

Far too much intimacy and commitment required here, says everyone knowingly—so naturally you go all contrary and contract an arranged marriage with, say, a Tibetan sherpa or an Inuit sealer, and stay faithful (you are a fixed sign), although of course you never actually meet.

Aquarius in Love
cool, ironic, detached...

Love is a word loaded with a bit too much warm, sticky fuzzitude for you. Sure, you're very fond of all of us, particularly the wackos, in a general way, but you're not keen on individuals, who tend to cling and whine and ask if you really, really love them, when all you want is to be left alone with your manga novels. You occasionally get infatuated (some humans are just so cute), but as a rational being soon work out that it is all about hormones and body language mirroring and it will go away. Being thought obvious and corny is the worst thing that could ever happen to you, so even if you did fall truly, madly, deeply, etc., no one would ever know from your cool, ironic, detached swagger.

Stalker?
Pro. There's nothing you like better than observing your lover closely from afar; in fact, that's as near as you like to get.

Tease?
Not on purpose, but you can't help blowing cold when they blow hot, and vice versa, so it's the same difference.

Gold digger?
The reverse. Money is vulgar and obvious; you go for the dirt poor and indigent so that you can feel superior.

Waterboy pickup lines

You are way too cool for conventional small talk, so you try to fascinate by:
- Swishing about in your long, black leather coat and shades
- Talking only in Estonian
- Going to sleep

Dating Aquarius
quite contrary

Amazingly you always get a date, or at least a close encounter of some kind, because there is always somebody, somewhere, who goes for the oddball (this is rarely another Aquarian, because they won't think you're odd at all). Dating you is not for the faint-hearted because you can't stop yourself acting contrary, so always turn up in bermudas and boxing boots for a Black and White Ball, or in a tux and Guccis for a yard sale, and bring along a megaphone and a small, stuffed 'gator to the first dinner with the parents.

You love speed-dating—it is the most efficient mating ritual you have come across on this planet—but are so unnervingly interested in everybody that people don't check your box, unless they are Virgo and want to knock themselves out trying to bring you into line.

People who are on a break from Mr./Ms. Sensible can find you hanging around Trekkie fests, IT seminars, cult recruitment drives, downtown Roswell, NM, Republican fundraisers, soup kitchens, or any university physics block with a decent particle accelerator.

Dates should get used to the fact that it won't be just you two, for that brings on your claustrophobia. When you say double date, you mean one you and three them. This is not as exciting as it sounds. After an evening at your fetish club *du jour* (last year it was the one where everyone dressed up in furry animal suits), or maybe a movie (*Eraserhead* or *Oklahoma!*—you hate to be predictable), you all end up playing short chess with the condiment sets in an all-nite diner. If you ever get to a third date—well, you're always up for it—you all go to one of their places, because you are living in Box City, for research purposes. You always call, but about a year later.

Romance Levels

— incandescent

— burning

— hot

— warm

— cool

— cold

— sub-zero

Aquarius love token

This scares you, because gift giving in most cultures is the trigger for some sort of intimacy power play and you may get trapped. Get around it by handing over something so weird they give it straight back: a snowglobe of the Mojave desert, perhaps, or a pickled ear (not necessarily your own).

Aquarius online

This is your favorite. A glass wall between you and the universe is comfy normality for you. You're free to be any body/age/species, and poke and prod and manipulate human emotions without copping any messy bloodspatter. They'll never catch up with you—you're far too much of an übergeek to leave any digital footprints. You'd prefer to be online permanently, so try to lure potential dates into a Wi-Fi zone, hook them up to one of your spare laptops, and clatter away on iChat while you sit side by side in silence.

What gets Aquarius hot

Robocop. Dressing up as a different species, so you can peep out from behind the mask without revealing a stupid coital grin. Floating, effortless, sweat-free, zero-G sex. A Venusian mind meld. Observing and being observed. How great would it be to have sex dressed in motion capture suits and watch yourself in CGI? If none of the above, you can always get off going online to World of Warcraft, and boning a Draenei Warrior Queen in your avatar as a Blood Elf Paladin.

Between the sheets

Let's get this over with. Your ruling planet is Uranus, ha ha ha; that does not mean you are obliged to act on a juvenile pun, but you do, along with all the other known positions and body combos, because every good scientist needs empirical data. They are all a bit too touchy-feely for you; your favorite is phone sex, where you talk your way to satisfaction, or the hot new rave from Japan, air sex—think air guitar—all the action without body contact and having to pretend you care afterwards.

Sex with Aquarius

remote and controlled

A software glitch means you have no direct feed linking sensation to brain. There's always a time lag, giving you the chance to evaluate sense data as they come in, decide whether or not you're having fun, and delete the dull parts. You never have emotionally unprotected sex or get swept away by lust, and there's always time to write up your notes as you're going along (try not to let partners catch you doing this). This means you are always in control, which is good; but it also means you get bored and fidgety waiting for partners to come down off the ceiling, or wake up. If you haven't already installed a spycam, why not pass the time by drilling a hole through to the neighbor's bedroom to see how they do it? Or invite a few friends around, try some themes and variations? Even better, dress up in each other's underwear and play *Invasion of the Body Snatchers*.

Aquarius and Mars

As you have seen (*see page 9*), Mars is the planet of sweaty individual action, and wherever it is in your birthchart signals how down and dirty you are prepared to go to get what you want. Because you are the sign of intellect and distance, if Mars is in Aquarius as well as your Sun, the answer is not very far, so lovers expecting to be flown to the Moon on gossamer wings had better bring their own rocket boosters.

Aquarius sex toys

Restraints (they remind you of liftoff) or anything remote-control, but what you really want is an orgasmatron, the one-person walk-in orgasm inducer last seen in Woody Allen's *Sleeper*.

163

Incompatibility Charts

aquarius vs. the rest

Brightsiders say that Aquarius (masculine, Air, fixed, perverse) gets along best with other Air signs who'll understand (Gemini and Libra), and worst with Taurus, Leo, and Scorpio (the other fixed signs who don't do compromise). However, this is the Darkside, where everybody is incompatible with everyone else. Here's how.

Aquarius and Aries You've always got an Aries or two stalking you because they can't resist that hard-to-get thing. Don't threaten them with a shotgun; they'll just want you even more.

Aquarius and Taurus A fixed sign like you, so playing cold and remote until –they lose interest won't work, because they'll never lose interest in anything they have set their heart and hooves on.

Aquarius and Gemini. A fellow Air sign, so you're safe from any sticky intimacy, but it won't stop them smiling into your eyes at the end of the evening while they palm your credit card.

Aquarius and Cancer They know it's just a difficult teenage phase you're going through (you're 32) and forgive you everything. You'll have to behave really, really, really badly to get out of this one.

Aquarius and Leo A fixed sign and your opposite. They want Hollywood and Oscars and you want Sundance and Palme d'Or, so Irreconcilable Artistic Differences end it all on the first date.

Aquarius and Virgo You like a logical system, but you like your independence more, so you sneak out of the soy bar and skip town while they are very kindly rediarizing your laptop for you.

164

Aquarius and Libra Mucho air kissing all around (they are the cardinal Air sign), but they're from Venus whereas you're not, so it will only last as long as you make them look cool.

Aquarius and Scorpio A fellow fixed sign; they can't resist the perverse, and bring whips and scourges on the third date, but you hate to be predictable, so turn up wearing your Silver Ring.

Aquarius and Sagittarius This is great because everybody wonders what an ultra-cool cat like you is doing with the zodiac's big, boisterous dog—and you love keeping them guessing.

Aquarius and Capricorn They are so straight you can stop trying quite so hard to be a recalcitrant rebel, because simply turning up on a date in Havaianas is enough to cause entertaining outrage.

Aquarius and Aquarius You are sitting in a boho coffee shop pointedly ignoring each other; tidy-minded Virgo set you up, because they figured you should go for another oddball. Wrong!

Aquarius and Pisces Emotional blackmail—the fish manipulation method of choice—won't work, on account of you having no emotions, so they wriggle away before the drinks tab comes.

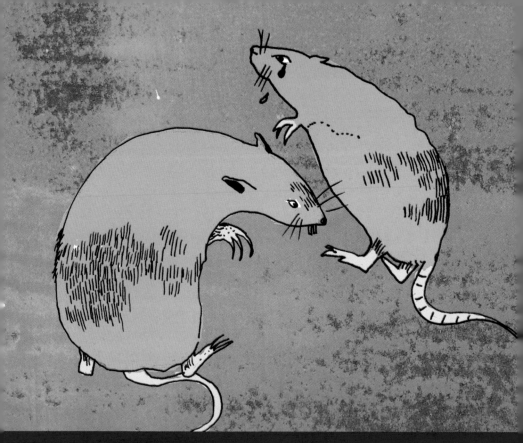

Love rat?

Rat on a wheel. When lovers get clingy
and dependent, you get cool and detached
and emotionally unavailable; the more they
demand from you, the further you step
aside. So they give up and become cool and
detached themselves, which is when you find
them irresistible and come on hot and strong;
so they get clingy and dependent, and you
get cool and detached and emotionally
unavailable ... this one could run and run.

GETTING BACK AT AQUARIUS

Every trick you try they see as
interesting, and call you to discuss
motive and methodology. Out them as
closet normals. Photoshop® snaps of
them cruising the aisles in Wal-Mart
and post them on their Web ring; sign
them up to a Celine Dion fanzine; tell
their mom where they live.

Your Cheatiŋ' Heart

in theory

This is all a bit academic in your case, because for cheating to occur there has to be a meaningful relationship of some kind, and you are always careful not to let anything messy like that develop, explaining calmly with infuriating logic that no one owns another person and we are all free to do as we like—especially you. Is it your fault the rest of the zodiac is driven by relic brain behavior? When you do "cheat," it's either online or an affair that you think will not threaten the status quo. You are always genuinely surprised when it does and people come at you with a gat or a tire iron. And you really, really do not understand why, when you say, "But honey, he/she means nothing to me," your lover gets even madder. When dumped, you take no notice, or think of it as an interesting opening gambit to a whole new game.

Aquarius excuses

You don't do excuses, but are always ready to explain, "I missed our anniversary dinner because I met someone more interesting in the bar and went home with them instead." When you say, "I need more space," you mean exactly that, but no one believes you.

Aquarian pre-nup

This is like diplomatic immunity and made up entirely of get-out clauses and guarantees that you have never had—or ever will have—any personal liability for anything. Even then you wouldn't sign it, but present your own biodegradable version, in Sanskrit or COBOL, carved into a wedge of Monterey Jack or written in woad on tree bark (from a sustainable source) so that it fades away when you do.

Venus and Aquarius

opposites attract

You and Venus go together like two things that really don't go together. Her MO is to play with senses and emotions until we are all mindless with desire and physical abandon, but you don't do mindless or physical abandon, so she spends quite a lot of her time with you pouting in the corner. Contrarily, you find her very attractive when she backs off like that. Astrological logistics (*see pages 8–9*) mean that your Venus will be in Aquarius, Sagittarius, Capricorn, Pisces, or Aries.

Hot Aquarius Role Models

James Dean, February 8, 1931
How hard-to-get cool do you want to play it? Professional rebel without a cause, mean, moody, magnificent, and elusive of gender, died young and pretty.

Colette, January 28, 1873
Rebellious, convention-busting, bisexual French novelist, keen on subverting stereotypes; creator of *Claudine* (1900), the sweet, saucy schoolgirl, and *Cheri* (1920), the pearl-draped boy toy.

Venus in Aquarius

Venus in Aquarius, when you are already Aquarius, makes you the Ice Queen everyone lusts after, but no one can get anywhere near. You can't be doing with all this physical neediness and up close and personal stuff; you like a partner who is online, in tight underwear, on the other side of the world, and preferably agoraphobic, so there's no danger of them ever coming to visit.

Venus in Sagittarius

Venus warms you up a few degrees in this nonchalant position; or perhaps it's just friction burn from the ropes you use to lash yourself to your partner for your sex 'n' skydiving sessions. You stay cool all the way down, and have never missed the ground yet.

Venus in Capricorn

This is the hard-hearted muse-with-an-MBA placing. Because you are coolly desirable, scientific geniuses, cult novelists, rock stars, and conceptual artists flock to you; you gain a layer of celeb gloss and, when they're rich, famous, and dead, you take over the estate as well as the royalties.

Venus in Pisces

When Venus swims with the fish it means emotional manipulation—in this case, of the slippery, cold-hearted kind. Overconfident types think you are a crushable pushover until you go kissing and telling on Montel.

Venus in Aries

This position gives extra thrust to your rocket boosters, so you burn hot and cold. You snap the action on your cellphone camera and send hotshots direct to your lover, who will be dumped by the time they pick them up. You must move on, but it will give them something to remember you by—as will the rash.

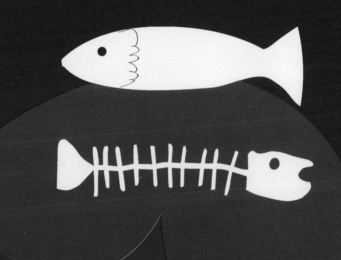

Pisces

February 19–March 20

Dreamy, directionless, sentimental, oversensitive plant in search of unlimited TLC, unconditional love and affection, and a free ride; as a highly talented (Pulitzer Prize) creative (retrospective at MoMA) and caring (former advisor to Mother Theresa) human being, I would love to enjoy the finer things in life, but have been ground down by other people's petty spite and the malicious withholding of funds by my bank. If you have a big horse, shining armor, a fat billfold, and promise never to criticize or judge, call me and let me tell you one of my life stories over a case of Margaux (your treat).

One-night stand

You only have one of these when you are already in a relationship (or possibly two). It's strictly medicinal, you're stressed out, they don't understand or love you enough, so it's all their fault you have to seek the comfort of strangers—often several times a night.

Two-year stretch

This is a long time in the same fishbowl, and will only work if you are both in a correctional facility or rehab, or they lock you in a fully serviced penthouse suite at the Chateau Marmont. Even then, you'll get engaged to at least two other people before your release date.

Long-haul

This requires application and a grip on reality, or your partner to be in a Persistent Vegetative State (so you can rack up some quality self-sacrifice points). However, having someone in house to blame for everything and to scrapbook your suicide notes is very tempting.

Pisçes in Love

falling in love, again

Call you a sentimental, romantic fool, but you're always in love—just not with the same person as you were five minutes ago, because they were mean to you and asked for their credit card back. You are too fragile for this world; it's too emotionally draining on your sensitive little soul to do any work on existing relationships that go a bit wrong, so you smile bravely, move on, and find someone new who really cherishes the supersensitive inner you and doesn't make hurtful remarks about your lost weekends. This is it: you start choosing flatware patterns. Then, across the crowded bar you spot a new love, who looks like they might understand you even more generously.

Stalker?

Not as such, but you love to doormat yourself in front of cruel lovers, to show the world how hard done by you are.

Tease?

Your mind changes every 7.5 seconds and you have no short-term memory. Who knows what you mean when you say yes?

Gold digger?

Of course. You can't hold down a job and your bar tab equals the GNP of Japan. Anyway, the world owes you a living.

Fish pickup lines

Emotional blackmail is your signature seduction technique; winners include:
- ♥ I've only got six months to live
- ♥ My girlfriend's in a coma
- ♥ I just flew in from Iraq

Dating Pisces
feel the need

Despite being a pile of wet Kleenex®, you always get a date because you're shrewd enough to realize that there's a whole market to exploit out there if you don't insist on alpha. You know, on daytime cable, when butt-ugly bottom-feeders come on and talk about their rich and complicated sex lives and we all ask ourselves how? Why? Pisces is the answer. You target the sick, ugly, outcast, or psychologically damaged because you think they will be pathetically grateful and eager to fulfill some of your many needs: constant unconditional affection, someone else's emotional depths to wallow in, and a chance to be codependent—your lifestyle of choice.

Splashing around in the Z-list tank is not your only option. Speed-dating suits your tiny attention span, but you always turn up late or at the wrong venue because no one reminded you. And if you do make it, you dither about so long deciding which box to check that you end up dating the cleaning crew who come around to lock up. People with an emotional deathwish can always find you cruising bars, empathizing at support group meetings for sordid conditions you don't have, or in the confessional.

You arrange to meet in your favorite murky bar—you're always an hour late or have been there three days already—where you don't let them get a drink in edgeways as you tell them how misunderstood you are, stare into their eyes, and sob that they are the one.

You'll get to third date because you are a limpet, you've made them feel sorry for you, or you've stolen their key. You always go to their place (visitors aren't allowed at the clinic, and it's a chance to case the joint). You won't call back, because you have lost your cellphone.

incandescent

burning

hot

warm

cool

cold

sub-zero

Pisces love token

This will always be something someone else has given you that you don't want any more, or something you shoplifted. You always say you give your heart, and ask, wet-eyed, if that is not enough—well, no, it isn't; not when it's on elastic so that you can pull it back whenever you want to.

Pisces online

Where else can you spend all day reframing reality to suit your ever-changing requirements? You can be whoever you feel like, fantasize all you like (and that's a lot), post photos on match.com of what you think you look like—or would have looked like, if Mom had paid for the nose job you wanted—and tell all those pointless lies you love: claiming you had sushi for lunch, when all the time you had tuna melt, announcing that you are dying of radiation sickness, etc., without anyone getting lintpicky about it.

What gets Pisces hot

Because your life is one long fantasy anyway, it's a very small step to the sexual kind that makes you even wetter than you already are. It's all about degradation and slavishness; being lashed to the bedpost with your own fishnets and forced to drink dirty Martinis, shuffling around on your hands and knees with your leash in your mouth playing Bad Doggy to Strict Master; anything that takes control away from you so that you can relax and blame everyone else if it all goes wrong.

Between the sheets

No-one knows what your favorite position is as you change your mind so often; partners who turn up all ready for Goat up a Tree (last week's hot maneuver) are spat on as insensitive and accused of playing away (where else could they have picked up such a disgusting move?). Sitting positions leave your hands free for pouring and corkscrew handling. Anything where someone else does all the work always goes down well, and you can blame them when you fall asleep.

Sex with Pisces

baiting the line

Sex with you is a gamble; quite apart from your chronic NSU (you don't want to cure it, you won't be sick and interesting any longer), no one knows when you might holler roofies because you have changed your mind—again—and you love being a victim (all that attention and cute CSIs swabbing your DNA).

Of course you can do sex—you're good 'n' bendy, and 90 seconds is about as long as you can focus on anything—but as far as you're concerned, it's just the bait to catch punters unawares and trick them into saying they love you (easily done in the heat of the moment, unless they're Scorpio). Then you've got them, and can whine and wheedle, and manipulate and pile on the emotional blackmail to your heart's content (but you said you loved me), and leave them scrabbling about in your nets while you drift off to hook another sucker or two.

Pisces and Mars

As you have learned (*see page 9*), Mars is planet hard-and-fast, and wherever it is panting in your birthchart indicates how much burning love you can deliver. Sadly, you are the sign of nebulous-and-slow, which means that you are the wet blanket to Mars's towering inferno. If your Mars is in Pisces as well as your Sun, all of you are going to need a cosmic dosage of little blue pills to get you up and about.

Pisces sex toys

Twelve-inch stilettos and mink toe rings for your fetish friends, and a Rubber Duck vibrator for the bath—cute, wobbly, and wet, just like you.

Incompatibility Charts

pisces vs. the rest

Brightsiders say that Pisces (feminine, Water, mutable, fantasist) gets along best with other Water signs who'll understand (Cancer and Scorpio), and worst with Gemini, Virgo, and Sagittarius (the other mutable signs who worship inconsistency). However, this is the Darkside, where everybody is incompatible with everyone else. Here's how.

Pisces and Aries They are leader of the pack and you are holding out for a hero, of any gender. Aries should think about what actually happened to the leader of the pack before signing up.

Pisces and Taurus They fund your rehab sessions and give you everything you want, so of course you cheat on them, then sue when they trample you into fishmeal in a jealous rage.

Pisces and Gemini A fellow mutable sign, so understands about the mood swings and takes you out to meet a connection of theirs who can help you; it would be rude not to take advantage.

Pisces and Cancer A fellow Water sign; out of solidarity you work so hard making them feel useless and inadequate that there's no time left for self-pity of your own; that's the kind of fish you are.

Pisces and Leo You are the zodiac's clingy sycophant, but don't get above yourself. If they suspect you're not being sincere, it will get unpleasant. Remember how cats feel about fish.

Pisces and Virgo A mutable sign and your opposite; if you let them think they are in control, you can cajole any number of Rolexes out of them; it's when they want them back that you're in doo-doo.

Pisces and Libra You try to get it on—after all, you have scales in common (sorry!), and you too can be a charmer—but it's over when they find out you have no money, or at least none of your own.

Pisces and Scorpio A fellow Water sign, but fixed; you're their natural prey, always ready to throw yourself into a pit of degradation without being asked; after all, none of it will be your fault.

Pisces and Sagittarius A mutable sign, Fire to your Water; a terrifying dating combo for bar owners everywhere, because you drink the place dry, they set fire to it, then you both skip town.

Pisces and Capricorn This is a bit like going to dinner with your dad: a side order of disapproval with every tequila, unless the goat gnaws through its rope, then you both disappear for six days.

Pisces and Aquarius You hook up at a party in an altered state and become New Best Friends. You split when the drugs wear off, and they find out that you think the stars are God's daisy chain.

Pisces and Pisces Meltdown. After only one date you'll both be found, emotionally drained, in a spreading pool of cheap red wine and self-pitying negativity. It was all their fault.

Love rat?

Supreme ratarama. If things get the least bit difficult—people trying to control you by expecting you to come home at night occasionally—or you feel slightly under pressure (your partner asks you what you want for dinner and forgets to tell you what you don't like), or if a better offer swims by, you simply drift off, leaving partners, children, debtors, etc. to tread water. You never feel guilty or look back because it is always someone else's fault.

GETTING BACK AT PISCES

Don't pander. If you retaliate or stop their allowance, they will feel deliciously used and sorry for themselves, which is what they like best. Call their office and tell their coworkers which bar they're in when they're off sick, just to make you feel better, then ignore them forever. They can't cope with lack of attention.

Your Cheatin' Heart

look what you made me do

Even when caught with your pants down, in midthrust in your partner's best friend's bed, with Marvin Gaye on the MP3 and a plate of half-eaten oysters on the floor, you deny everything. It's not what it looks like. You fell out of a passing 747 brought unexpectedly low by turbulence; you were on your way to Scranton, NJ, to visit a sick aunt who craves oysters—how kind are you. The partner's best friend Rohypnoled your Sprite. You did it for your partner; you didn't want to upset their best friend, who was begging for it. Anyway it's your partner's fault for getting so fat you had to go elsewhere; besides, you thought the relationship was an open one, because they once said they had a thing for Brad Pitt. When dumped, you sulk and bitch, and get other people to buy you drinks, then tell them how cruelly you've been treated.

Pisces excuses

There are five standard Pisces excuses, which, with some customizing and embellishment, can be used to cover every eventuality. 1) No, I didn't, it's all in your head; 2) It's not my fault; 3) You/they made me do it; 4) It's all your fault; 5) I'm not feeling well.

Pisces pre-nup

This is the size of an airport bonkbuster, because you change your mind every few seconds and have to cross out clauses and insert amendments. (You don't care, you're sleeping with your attorney, so it's all free.) The pre-nup grants you unlimited lying facilities, global immunity from the consequences of anything you do or say, and custody of the liquor cabinet, but you usually leave it in a downtown bar.

Venus and Pisces

sister act

While your manipulating skills are good, they're not quite in Venus's class, but she feels a bond (she was born on a half shell, after all). She is the queen of the cool girls, and you are her pet wannabe, despite your tendency to fall into the punchbowl at the prom. When you're together, the rest of us feel we are being played by a mother-and-daughter grifting scam, but don't quite know how. Astrological logistics (*see pages 8–9*) mean that your Venus will be in Pisces, Capricorn, Aquarius, Aries, or Taurus.

Hot Pisces Role Models

Jack Kerouac, March 12, 1922
Author of *On the Road* (1947), the definitive Piscean how-to manual of drift, drink, drugs, bad sex with the wrong people, and long, pointless, disorganized journeys made for no apparent reason.

Jean Harlow, March 3, 1911
The gorgeous but doomed "Platinum Blonde" bombshell, who only drifted into the Hollywood dream factory to please her mother's unfulfilled ambition.

Venus in Pisces

Venus in Pisces, when you are already Pisces, makes you soft, helpless, and supermanipulative, like a basket of kittens in a creamery. Adrift on a sea of schmaltz, you cling to your lover like a limpet with dependency issues, and overload the fragile rowboat of love with a cargo of kitsch. When a luxury cruise liner passes in the night, you jump ship.

Venus in Capricorn

Venus in this position keeps your ducks in a row; although you may woo your lover with rose-tinted lyrics and a treacly guitar solo, you keep copies and copyright, so you clean up on the lucrative T-shirt/mug/mouse pad/refrigerator magnet market.

Venus in Aquarius

This is the coy carp position, combining Aquarian cool and DILLIGAF attitude with Piscean dithering and Venusian determination. You hover in the mid-distance looking fetching behind a sea cucumber, then dart away like a startled fawn when they get near, so they are forced to lure you out of your grotto with shiny things from Tiffany's.

Venus in Aries

This is the *Jaws* placing. Suck in your swim bladder, stiffen your dorsal fin, and predate on all the pretty young fish, surfers, and stray dogs in the Atlantic. When you've done enough maiming and devouring, power off to your feeding grounds in the Pacific.

Venus in Taurus

Venus is in one of her own signs here, so overrides your tendency to let things slide and shows you how to get what you want and keep hold of it. This mainly involves lashing lovers to you with high-tensile fishing line, and making them dive for buried treasure.

Instant Blind-Date Identifier

You're on a blind date, or a first date with someone you picked up and can't remember where. Wouldn't it be good to find out in the first few minutes if it's going to be worth a couple of hours of your life? You don't want to do anything flaky, like asking them when their birthday is, in case they think you're interested. If you go in for big handbags, stuff this book in your tote and consult it underneath the table; if you want to be more discreet, run off a copy of these pages and keep them in your pocket to look at when your BD is at the bar.

How does it work?

The identifier is based on observed elemental energy. This is not as woo-woo as it sounds. There are four elements: Fire, Earth, Air, and Water; each element appears in four zodiac signs, but in three slightly different ways: in cardinal signs (Aries, Cancer, Libra, Capricorn) it erupts in its raw unadulterated state; in fixed signs (Taurus, Leo, Scorpio, Aquarius) it comes on as relentless and implacable; and in mutable signs (Gemini, Virgo, Sagittarius, Pisces) it is unpredictable and unstable, like a rogue WMD.

Once you have nailed the element, you can refine the search by asking various questions until you pinpoint which sign you're dealing with. Consult the Incompatibility Chart for your sign and see just how much you two won't get along, then decide whether to stick out the whole two hours or suddenly recollect a pressing engagement.

Identifying elements

The four elements have distinctive behavior patterns, which you can easily learn to recognize. Let's say you arrange to meet in a café-bar. Slide in discreetly so they don't catch you and study their general behavior. Don't try too hard—first impressions are what counts; at this stage it's the overall picture that's important.

----

1 Are they standing at the bar, constantly fidgeting, taking up a lot more space than they need, talking at other people, laughing loudly at their own jokes, flipping beer coasters, shuffling their feet, impatiently drumming their fingers on the bar counter?
Your BD is a FIRE sign:
go to panel 1, page 186.

2 Are they sitting at one of the better tables, studying the menu and their pocket calculator, scarfing down the free nibbles? Have they put their bag and neatly folded coat on the seat opposite to mark out their territory?
Your BD is an EARTH sign:
go to panel 2, page 187.

3 Are they perched on a bar stool, gabbling into their cell, pecking at their BlackBerry®, playing advanced Tetris® on their Nintendo DS™, reading Sin City, Skinny Bitch, or Magic for Dummies, or just smiling at themselves in the bar mirror.
Your BD is an AIR sign:
go to panel 3, page 188.

4 Are they sitting in a dark, easily defensible booth way off in the corner, with their back to the wall and a barricade of some kind in front of them? Or can you not see anyone who fits their description in the bar?
Your BD is a WATER sign:
go to panel 4, page 189.

PANEL 1 FIRE SIGNS

The zodiac's three Fire signs are: Aries, Leo, and Sagittarius. To find out which one yours might be, ask yourself the following questions:

Q
- Are they still wearing their work clothes (including the hard hat and cement dust)?
- Have they already had an argument with the bar staff, so that you have to leave as soon as you get there?
- When you get thrown out, do their bar buddies come with you? And hang around?

A
If the answer to all of these is Yes, your BD is 99 percent likely to be ARIES.
The clincher: They drive you around at high speed looking for their favorite rib shack, run a red light, and are busted by the cops; it isn't actually their car, so you have to stand bail, or spend the night in the lockup.

Q
- Are they wearing glittery clothes and keep fiddling with their hair?
- Have they already ordered your drink for you, and is it gold-colored with lots of parasols?
- Is their cellphone screensaver a self-portrait?

A
If the answer to all of these is Yes, your BD is 99 percent likely to be LEO.
The clincher: You go to their favorite restaurant (you get no choice), where everyone greets them like royalty, and you with a pitying smile. They tell you what you want to eat and spend the evening fielding calls from their agent.

Q
- Are they wearing a baseball cap backward, carrying a snowboard, or covered in Band-Aids®?
- Are they by mistake in the bar on the opposite side of the street because they wrote the details on the back of their hand and it washed off in their buddy's jacuzzi?
- Do they knock over your drink, order another one, then drink it themselves?

A
If the answer to all of these is Yes, your BD is 99 percent likely to be SAGITTARIUS.
The clincher: It takes them half an hour to get to you because they are best friends with everyone in the bar; when they are about 10 feet away they shout out merrily that you look way older than you do in your picture on the dating site.

PANEL 2 EARTH SIGNS

The zodiac's three Earth signs are: Taurus, Virgo, and Capricorn. To find out which one yours might be, ask yourself the following questions:

Q
• Are they wearing leather?
• Have they ordered a bottle of good red and are already halfway through it?
• Are they very antsy if you're fashionably late because it's 10 minutes past their usual feeding time?

A
If the answer to all of these is Yes, your BD is 99 percent likely to be TAURUS.
The clincher: The evening seems to go on very much longer than the two hours it actually takes up. They come on like you're after the Ring of Power if you ask to taste their tournedos Rossini, but have no problem eating half your dessert.

Q
• Are they wearing a T-shirt from 100 percent Fairtrade organic biodegradable cotton with an accusatory slogan on it?
• Are they cleaning the table with their own wet wipes?
• Are they drinking herbal tea or a double skinny soya?

A
If the answer to all of these is Yes, your BD is 99 percent likely to be VIRGO.
The clincher: They give you a copy of a detailed agenda for the evening that they created on Excel, and have brought an umbrella (it's summer) and some rice cookies because they are wheat-intolerant. You spend half the evening working out how the check splits.

Q
• Are they wearing a formal suit?
• Are they drinking tap water?
• Is the first thing they give you a business card?

A
If the answer to all of these is Yes, your BD is 99 percent likely to be CAPRICORN.
The clincher: You go to a franchise restaurant because they have vouchers on a two-for-one deal on the special menu before 8.30. You spend the rest of the evening playing "My APR is lower than yours" with your credit cards.

PANEL 3 AIR SIGNS

The zodiac's three air signs are: Gemini, Libra, and Aquarius. To find out which one yours might be, ask yourself the following questions:

Q
• Are they wearing labels they don't look like they can afford?
• Will they not let you get a word in edgeways?
• Have they ordered a bottle of Dom Perignon Rosé on your tab?

A
If the answer to all of these is Yes, your BD is 99 percent likely to be GEMINI.
The clincher: Three other candidates turn up just after you, and your BD can explain everything, but has just remembered they have to be in night court to sort out a minor retail-related misunderstanding. You and the other three go clubbing.

Q
• Have they hung their jacket up so that you can see its Prada?
• Do they smile a lot, but look constantly over your shoulder for someone more attractive to talk to?
• Are they drinking a very expensive cocktail sent over by someone on the other side of the bar?

A
If the answer to all of these is Yes, your BD is 99 percent likely to be LIBRA.
The clincher: They sit just a bit too close to you, laugh at the jokes even you know are pathetic, and call you "darling" and "sweetie" all night long because they have forgotten your name. Somehow you ended up paying, but you can't work out how.

Q
• Are they wearing odd socks or shoes, or a light-reflecting vest?
• Are they building a small model of Capitol Hill/the Millennium Falcon/Stonehenge out of ice blocks and toothpicks?
• Are they drinking something weird—Guinness with a green-tea chaser, for example?

A
If the answer to all of these is Yes, your BD is 99 percent likely to be AQUARIUS.
The clincher: After they introduce the three other dates they invited along, you all spend the evening sharing pizzas around their laptop, signing online petitions demanding action on climate change, Big Pharma legislation, and krill rights.

PANEL 4 WATER SIGNS

The zodiac's three Water signs are: Cancer, Scorpio, and Pisces. To find out which one yours might be, ask yourself the following questions:

Q

• Are they actually there, or is there a message for you behind the bar saying they can't come because it's all a dreadful mistake—and you wouldn't like them anyway?
• Have they brought their comfort blanket?
• Are they drinking chocolate malt?

A

If the answer to all of these is Yes, your BD is 99 percent likely to be CANCER.
The clincher: Their mom calls at least three times, and not only do they take the calls, but they tell you who it is and answer all her questions about you. Then they go to the restroom and don't come back until the bar closes.

Q

• Are they dressed in very neat black?
• Have they been there for half an hour, and has everyone else moved slightly further down the bar?
• Are they drinking triple espressos with no sugar?

A

If the answer to all of these is Yes, your BD is 99 percent likely to be SCORPIO.
The clincher: All you can remember is looking into their eyes, and then it all goes blank. You have no recollection of what you did or where you went, when you wake up safe in your own bed, alone apart from the handcuff key.

Q

• Do they look like they're wearing somebody else's clothes?
• Are they under the table?
• Does the barkeeper ask you to settle their tab before you can get another drink?

A

If the answer to all of these is Yes, your BD is 99 percent likely to be PISCES.
The clincher: They insist you go to a little bar just around the corner where everybody knows their name and loves them, but can't find it, blame you, burst into tears, and borrow $10 to get home.

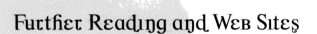

Further Reading and Web Sites

Here are some books and Web sites that you might like to check out. They are not exclusively Darkside, but most of them acknowledge its presence.

Books

Astrology and Difficult Relationships: Why are you in my life?, Beverly A. Flynn, TLH Publishing Company, 2006

Astrologically Incorrect: Unlock the secrets of the signs to get what you want when you want!, Terry Marlowe, Adams Media Corporation, 2003

How to Spot a Bastard by his Sun Sign: The Ultimate Horrorscope, Adele Lang and Susi Rajah, St. Martin's Press, 2002

Love on a Rotten Day: An Astrological Survival Guide to Romance, Hazel Dixon-Cooper, Fireside, 2004

The Mars/Venus Affair: Astrology's Sexiest Planets, Wendell Perry and Linda Perry, Llewellyn Publications, 2000

Sexscope: How to seduce, stimulate and satisfy any sign, Stuart Hazelton, Fireside, 2001

Sextrology: The Astrology of Sex and the Sexes, Stella Starsky and Quinn Cox, HarperCollins, 2004

Web sites

Astrodienst: *www.astro.com*
Combines top astrologists with state-of-the-art software to bring free horoscopes, links, shopping, etc.

Astrolabe: *www.alabe.com*
Free computer-generated birthcharts, as well as lots of other good stuff. Offers a standardized interpretation and should be used as a starter guide.

Astrology online: *www.astrology-online.com*
This site claims to be the largest astrology site on the Web and is certainly comprehensive and still growing.

Astrologyzine: *www.astrologyzine.com*
Free horoscopes, teach-yourself-astrology, and a lot about compatibility, love planets, and the Cupid Myth.

Astrolutely: *www.astrolutely.com*
Sassy stuff by Penny Thornton, once astrologer to Princess Diana. The Signs of Love section also includes the downside.

Café astrology: *www.cafeastrology.com*
A very stylish site, combining astrological know-how with fun; covers everything, including sexual astrology.

Sexual astrology: *www.sexualastrology.com*
This one is self-explanatory; very good on compatibility—or lack thereof.

Index

Acknowledgments

The author and publishers would like to thank the following for permission to reproduce photographs:

akg-images: 70b, 98b, 154b; Album: 84b, 182b, 56t. Art Archive/Culver Pictures: 28t; Fondation Thiers Paris/ Gianni Dagli Orti: 84t. Bridgeman Art Library/Private collection: 56b. Corbis/Claire Artman/zefa: 120; Bettmann: 28b, 126b, 154b, 182b; Roy Botterell: 162; Janni Chavakis/zefa: 36; Peter M. Fisher: 176; Lynn Goldsmith: 42t; Tim Graham: 70t; Douglas Kent Hall/Zuma: 140t; Hulton-Deutsch Collection: 98t, 126t; A. Inden/zefa: 106; Red James/zefa: 92; C. Lyttle/zefa: 50; Louis Moses/zefa: 78; Anthony Redpath: 134; Royalty-Free: 22, 148; Sunset Boulevard: 42b; Franco Vogt: 64; Jupiter Images: 112, 140.